Phenomenal Consciousness and Mind–Body Problem

Phenomenal Consciousness and Mind–Body Problem

in East–West Perspective

V.N. Misra

DK
PRINTWORLD
Publishers of Indian Traditions

Cataloging in Publication Data — DK
[Courtesy: D.K. Agencies (P) Ltd. <docinfo@dkagencies.com>]
Misra, V.N., author.
Phenomenal consciousness and mind-body problem in East-West perspective / VN Misra.
pages cm
Includes bibliographical references.

1. Consciousness. 2. Mind and body. 3. Phenomenology. 4. Philosophy of mind. 5. Hindu philosophy. I. Title.

LCC B808.9.M57 2018 | DDC 128.2 23

ISBN: 978-81-246-0946-0
First published in India in 2019

Printed and published by:
D.K. Printworld (P) Ltd.
Regd. Office: Vedaśrī, F-395, Sudarshan Park
(Metro Station: Ramesh Nagar), New Delhi - 110015
Phones: (011) 2545 3975, 2546 6019
e-mail: indology@dkprintworld.com
Website: www.dkprintworld.com

Preface

THIS study attempts to provide the solution to two problems of the Western philosophy: (i) the explanatory gap in the phenomenal consciousness; and (ii) the mind–body problem. The intentionality of consciousness and the mental causation having some bearings on the above problems are also discussed in the East–West perspective. The intentional consciousness is more or less similar to the phenomenal consiousness, whereas the mental causation would provide better understanding of the mind–body problem.

The gap in explaining the pheonomenal consciousness arises in the Western philosophy mainly because the distinction between the functions of consciousness and consciousness itself does not seem to have been perceived in proper perspective. In this context, it may be stated that consciousness which is embodied in human being is one. When it manifests or reflects, it becomes many. This fact has been realized in the Indian philosophy more than 2,000 years ago. More recently, an existentialist philospher Jean-Paul Sartre has evolved the concept of pre-reflective and reflective consciousness. These two are one consciousness because reflective consciousness depends upon pre-reflective consciousness.

If one realizes the pathway of reflection of consciousness, it would be easy to explain the phenomenal consciousness. In the Western philosophy the access consciousness is also discussed along with the phenomenal consciousness. According to Sartre, access consciousness is real because it is accessible to every human being. Therefore, it may be said that the phenomenal consciousness is the reflection of the access consciousness. In the approach, there is no explanatory gap in the phenomenal consciousness.

However, an attempt has also been made to explain the phenomenal consciousness through the higher-order thought. This approach does not seem to be appropriate because the higher-order thought happens to be the object of consciousness. In this context, it may be stated that according to Sartre, consciousness can be the only source of consciousness. If this view is accepted, it may be reassuringly to be told that the access consciousness happens to be the source of phenomenal consciousness. Therefore, there is no explanatory gap in the phenomenal consciousness. In the Indian philosophy also, there is no gap in experiencing phenomenal consciousness because it is treated as a menifestation or reflection of self-consciousness.

The mind–body problem arises in the Western philosophy mainly because the mind is treated as synonymous to consciousness. But it ought be recognized that the Western philosopher John R. Searle has solved the mind–body problem by differentiating the consciousness from mind. In that he has recognized the consciousness happens to be the first-person ontology, whereas the mind is the third-person ontology because it is identical to brain.

What is equally important is that even the quantum theory has solved the mind–body problem by admitting the connection between the mind and the body. It is stated that in the implicate order, mind enfolds matter in general and the body in particular. Similarly, the body enfolds not only mind but also in some sense the entire material universe. This in a way solved the mind–body problem.

On the basis of above observations, an inference may be drawn that those Western philosophers who are raising the mind–body problem, are not interested in solving the problem. Their main purpose seems to be that let this problem be a live one. However, an attempt has been made in this study to provide the solution to the mind–body problem based on not only the philosophical views of East and West but it has also included the solution based on the scientific reasoning.

I am, indeed grateful to Shri M.L. Pandit who always encouraged me to write books having bearing on philosophical problems. I am indebted to Dr S.M. Pathak, Dr S.K. Mishra, Shri S.K. Sharma, Shri P.R. Sharma and Shri A.B. Choudhury for their appreciation of my earlier books on philosophy.

I express my gratitude to the authors from whose works I have quoted passages across the chapters of this book.

I also express my gratitude to Shri Susheel K. Mittal, Director, D.K. Printworld, for two things: (i) sincere efforts in producing error-free and good quality books to the extent possible, and (ii) respectful attitude to the author.

V.N. Misra

Contents

Introduction

Two main problems: (i) explanatory gap in the phenomenal consciousness, and (ii) the mind–body problem have been discussed quite intensively during the last few decades in the Western philosophy.

An attempt has recently been made to explain the phenomenal consciousness through of higher-order thought. It may, however, be pointed out that the phenomenal consciousness or reflective consciousness and higher-order thought are the objects of consciousness itself, which are embodied in human being. This consciousness is generally known as self-consciousness because it manifests through mind, according to the Vedānta school of Indian philosophy. If the phenomenal consciousness is not treated as manifestation or reflection of self-consciousness, it is rather difficult to explain it.

The mind–body problem has risen in the Western philosophy mainly because consciousness and mind are treated as synonymous. However, J.R. Searle has solved the mind–body problem mainly because consciousness has been treated as first-person ontology. He has categorically stated that we cannot reduce consciousness to its neurobiological basis, because such a third-person reduction would leave out the first-person ontology of consciousness.[1]

This study attempts to provide the solution to both the problems: explanatory gap in the phenomenal consciousness and

[1] Searle, 2004, *Mind: A Brief Introduction*, p. 79.

the mind–body problem. This is mainly because both the problems are interconnected in the sense that self-consciousness which is responsible for the pathway of reflection of the phenomenal consciousness can also be the source under which the mind–body problem may be resolved. The study also discusses the intentionality and mental causation in East–West perspective. The former deals with the objective or external world, whereas the latter is mainly concerned with the subjective or inner sense. The intentionality and mental causation are expected to provide better understanding of the phenomenal consciousness and the mind–body problem.

I. Explanatory Gap in Phenomenal Consciousness

The source of phenomenal consciousness may be found in the consciousness itself. This may be explained through the pathway of reflection. It means that the self-consciousness exists in me, when it manifests, it becomes the phenomenal consciousness or reflective consciousness to be involved in the phenomenal world. If this basic fact is not accepted, it will be all the more difficult to explain the phenomenal consciousness. The pathway of reflection is explained as:

> A question about being is one that we pursue the pathway of reflection. The philosophy of being discovers its subject matter by bending back its attention to the awareness of being that we already possess, that is given us all with our life and breath. All human beings have an awareness of being — they are aware that they exist and that other people and other things exist. Attention to that awareness will guide the philosophy of being. A philosophy that pays heed to human awareness will discover, through reflection, the awareness of being that we have always had.[2]

It may be stated that consciousness and awareness are synonymous.[3]

Now let us see how the reflective consciousness has been

[2] Nicholson, 1962, *Illustration of Being*, p. 6.

[3] Dretske, 2002, "Conscious Experience", p. 422.

explained by the pre-reflective consciousness in the existential philosophy of Jean-Paul Sartre. Since by nature all consciousness is self-consciousness; the pre-reflective consciousness or non-thetic consciousness is also self-consciousness. As regards the reflective consciousness, it is also known as thetic consciousness or positional consciousness. However, the main difference between the pre-reflective and reflective consciousness is that in the former (i.e. pre-reflective consciousness) there is no ego, whereas the latter (i.e. reflective consciousness) contains ego. But the reflective consciousness cannot be separated from the pre-reflective consciousness. This is evident from the fact that the reflective consciousness of an object is at the same time the pre-reflective consciousness itself. The reflection has no primacy over the consciousness reflected on. It is the pre-reflective consciousness which becomes the basis of reflective consciousness.

It may, however, be stated that the pre-reflective consciousness and reflective consciousness are two different phases of the one and the same consciousness. These two successive phases — the first pre-reflective is the subjectivity, which transforms itself into the second phase of reflective consciousness, which reveals the objects involved in the phenomenal world.

If the above observations regarding the pre-reflective consciousness and reflective consciousness are taken into account, the phenomenal consciousness may be easily explained. But the fact of matter is that those who are found explanatory gap in the phenomenal consciousness, they are not interested in looking at other's observations in which there is no problem of explanatory gap in the phenomenal consciousness. Those who love their own experience, it is difficult for them to solve the problem of explanatory gap. It is rather a well-known fact that if there is any problem, its reconciliation may be possible only by looking at other's observations under which there is no explanatory gap in explaining the phenomenal consciousness. This is the most important not only for explanatory gap, but it is also important for knowing the truth;

for "the best way to consider truth is through the interplay of viewpoints: the interest of truth requires a diversity of opinions".[4]

It may be reassuringly to be told again that the consciousness cannot be divided, which is evident from the following observation:

> The consciousness, although it is a complex entity, is only one. When we speak of its "parts" or "divisions", the only thing that we want to indicate is that it has diverse activities, diverse forms of manifestations, in the empirical reality — empirical reality that is created by the same consciousness when it manifests itself. It is not a real concrete division; it is only a theoretical division, a product of the conceptual analysis.[5]

Now let us see how the manifestations of consciousness are taking place in the Indian philosophy of Advaita Vedānta and Yogācāra Vijñānavāda Buddhism.

II. Manifestation of Consciousness

Advaita Vedānta

When pure consciousness reflects in *antaḥkaraṇa* (the mind or internal organ), it is known as *cidābhāsa*, which gives rise to the ego (*ahaṁ*). This consciousness associated with the eternal organ is capable of reflection which takes place during our waking and dream experiences. "In our waking experience there is "I" which functions as knower (*jñātā*), as doer (*kartā*), and as experiencer (*bhoktā*): it functions, that is to say, as the subject of knowledge, as the agent of action and as the experiencer of the consequences of action".[6] This shows that the consciousness becomes intentional when it is associated with the mind.

However, the intentional consciousness is mostly associated

---

[4] Sarbadhikari, 1991, *Mill's Self Regarding Acts*, p. 4.

[5] Tola and Dragonetti, 2004, *Being as Consciousness*, p. 201.

[6] Balasubramanian, 2004, "*Advaita Vedanta on the Problem of Enworlded Subjectivity*", p. 84.

with "I" which limits the functioning of consciousness because it is tied up with objects, internal or external involved in the empirical world. In fact, it is stated:

> By cutting the knot of the ego, consciousness ceases to be personal, it is spread out infinitely, and becomes identical with the world which is a content of the transcendental consciousness – arising from it and again withdrawing into it. So long as consciousness is ego-centric, all thoughts, feelings and actions are directed towards furthering the interests of the ego. But when consciousness is universe-centric, thoughts and actions no longer serve the interests of a single individual, they become disinterested. As there can be no sense of want there is no longer any feeling of pleasure or pain: there is only a sense of fullness, unvarying and undying.[7]

All manifestations are based on duality: the knower and the known, the observer and the observed. This is created by the mind with a view to gain the experience from the empirical world. The mind is mainly capable of discursive knowledge which understands everything through differentiations and distinctions. Therefore, without creating duality in the sphere of knowledge, the mind cannot gain experience. The manifestations of consciousness take place mainly in the empirical world, which has only relative existence.

In the reflective consciousness, the mind is involved as an instrument. Therefore, consciousness in reflection becomes *pramātṛ* (knower).[8] It may be noted that Vedānta has also recognized the concept of *sākṣī-caitanya* (witness consciousness), which in itself does not decide about the right or wrong, its main function is to reflect its own light. In this context, the deciding factor happens to be *pramātṛ-caitanya* (knower).[9] However, in the reflection *pramātṛ-*

---

[7] Bhattacharyya, 2004, "Phenomenology and Indian Philosophy", p. 72.

[8] Swami Madhavananda, 2000, *Vedāntaparibhāṣā of Dharmarāja Adhvarīndra*, p. 14.

[9] Manju, 1986, *Advaitavāda aura Śūnyavāda*, p. 53.

caitanya is not separate from the witness consciousness: the former depends upon the latter. Whatever is known to *sākṣī-caitanya*, it also becomes known to *pramātṛ-caitanya*. The witness consciousness reflects the modifications of mind, which are unknown to *pramātṛ-caitanya*, but it is known to witness consciousness.[10] Therefore, an inference may be drawn that the reflective consciousness knows the objects mainly through the light which it receives from the witnessing consciousness (*sākṣī-caitanya*).

Self-consciousness has, however, been interpreted as *jīvātman* in the Vedāntic framework. It is stated that pure consciousness (i.e. *Brahman*) is manifesting in every human being as self-consciousness that is direct and intuitive. It is explained as:

> This is immutable consciousness (*kūṭastha*) ever present as the witness-self (*sākṣī*). It illuminates the mental states: pleasure, pain, hope, fear, knowledge, ignorance, love, hate, memory, loss of memory and so forth. The mental states are immediately cognized because of their presence to witness self. It is the immediacy of self awareness that makes an object immediately known. To be directly cognized, an object must be allied with luminous self. Knowledge is direct, i.e. perceptual, when the object is known directly. The immutable consciousness that the witness self is being reflected in the mind and apparently limited by it, appears as the ego, the empirical self, which functions as the percipient (*pramātā*).[11]

The above description of self-consciousness as *jīvātman* is fairly comparable to self-awareness (self-consciousness) treated as mental perception by Diṅnāga. In this case comprehension aspect of self-consciousness happens to be knowing subject, representing thereby as self in perception. This may be reassured by any other observation that "Self-consciousness is essentially a case of knowledge, it makes presence to us our own Self. It is

---

[10] Manju, 1986, op. cit., p. 53.

[11] Swami Satprakashananda, 2001, *Methods of Knowledge*, p. 91.

not a construction, it is not an illusion and therefore it is direct knowledge."[12] It has also been assured that without the doctrine of self-consciousness self-cognition) recollection is not possible.

Yogācāra Vijñānavāda Buddhism (Transformations of Consciousness: Ātman and Dharma)

The Absolute Reality happens to be pure consciousness and how it gets transformed into the duality in appearance of subjective and objective sides of experience, is explained below on the basis of the first verse of thirty stanzas (*Triṁśikā*):

> आत्मधर्मोपचारो हि विविधे यः प्रवर्तते।
> स विज्ञानपरिणामेसौ परिणामः स च त्रिधा।।1।।
>
> *ātmadharmopacāro hi vividhe yaḥ pravartate* ।
> *sa vijñanpariṇāmesau pariṇāmaḥ sa ca tridhā* ।।
>
> Whatever, indeed, is the variety of ideas of self and elements that prevails, it occurs in the transformation of consciousness. Such transformation is threefold.[13]

Self (*ātman*) and element (*dharma*) are treated as subjective and objective sides, respectively of experience.[14] In another interpretation, *ātman* is referred to as controlling power and *dharma* is used as a norm or support. The former may appear as sentient beings (*sattva*) or as living things (*jīva*), whereas the latter may appear as substance (*dravya*), qualities (*guṇas*), actions (*karmas*) and aggregates (*skandhas*).[15] The word *pravartate* (arising) signifies the appearances of self (*ātman*) and *dharmas*, which are produced by causes and conditions.[16]

---

[12] Stcherbatsky, 1996, *Buddhist Logic*, vol. II, p. 30.

[13] Kalupahana, 1992, op. cit., p. 192.

[14] Kochumuttom, 1999, *A Buddhist Doctrine of Experience*, p. 129.

[15] Ganguly, 1992, *Treatise in Thirty Verses on Mere Consciousness*, p. 76.

[16] Ibid.

Pariṇāma (transformation) indicates that:

> The substance (*saṁvitti bhāga*) of consciousness develops itself into two divisions (*bhāgas*), when it is produced, i.e. the perceived division (*nimitta-bhāga*) and the perceiving faculty (*darśana-bhāga*). These divisions arise out of another decision called self-witness, i.e. *svasaṁvitti-bhāga* which is their essential substance. On the basis of these two functional divisions, *ātman* and *dharma* are established.[17]

III. Mind–Body Problem

Descartes's Formula: "I Think Therefore I Am"

The mind–body problem has been started by Descartes 300 years ago in the Western philosophy. This problem has been realized by him in the sixth meditation in which it is observed:

> When the mind understands, it in some way turns towards itself and inspects one of the ideas which is within it; but when it imagines, it turns towards the body and looks at something in the body which conforms to an idea understood by the mind or perceived by the senses. I can, as I say, easily understand that this is how imagination comes about, if the body exists; and since there is no other equally suitable way of explaining imagination that comes to mind. I can make a probable conjecture that body exists. But this is only a probability; and despite a careful and comprehensive investigation I do not yet see how the distant idea of a corporal nature which I find in my imagination can provide any basis for a necessary inference that somebody exists.[18]

The above observation shows that the imagination provides the basis for necessary inference that body exists. However, the mind is thinking an unextended substance, whereas the body happens to be unthinkable an extended one.[19] The interaction between the

---

[17] Ganguly, 1992, op. cit., pp. 76-77.

[18] Descartes, 2002, "Meditations on First Philosophy", p. 14.

[19] Chakraborty, 1997, op, cit., p. 35.

mind and the body has been established by Descartes through soul, which "is joined to the whole body, and that we cannot properly say that it exists in any one part of the body to the exclusion on the others".[20] It is further stated that there is a little gland referred to as the pineal gland in the centre of the brain where the soul exercises its functions more particularly than in the other parts of the body. This is explained below:

> On carefully examining the matter I think I have clearly established that the part of the body in which the soul directly exercises its functions is not the heart at all, or the whole of the brain. It is rather the innermost part of the brain, which is a certain very small gland situated in the middle of the brain's substance and suspended above the passage through which the spirits in the brain's anterior cavities communicate with those in its posterior cavities. The slightest movements on the part of this gland may alter very greatly the course of these spirits, and conversely any change, however slight, taking place in the course of the spirits may do much to change the movements of the gland.[21]

The above observations indicate that the interaction has been established between the spirit and the body rather than the mind and the body. Does it mean that Descartes has used the spirit as synonymous to the mind? There is no clarity on this aspect. However, Descartes' idea about mind as thinking substance has been quite influential, yet it cannot be reduced to brain.[22] That apart, the fact remains that Descartes' ideas about the mind–body problem has been criticized by many. This has been summed up very well in the following critical assessment:

> Many objections have been raised to the idea that a non-physical mind controls the movement of physical body. It is not clear

[20] Descartes, 2002, op. cit, p. 21.

[21] Ibid., p. 22.

[22] Feinberg, 2001, *Altered Egos*, p. 139.

just how a non-physical substance and a physical substance can interact. The idea that the pineal gland mediates this interaction has long since been rejected on physiological grounds, and it is unclear whether any better causal nexus could exist. Further, it is often held that this interaction cannot be reconciled with physics, which postulates a closed network of physical interactions, with no room for a non-physical mind to play any role.[23]

Sartre's Interpretation of Descartes's Formula: "I Think Therefore I Am"

The above formula has been criticized by Sartre on the following grounds:

i. The consciousness which says "I am" is not actually the consciousness which thinks. Instead we are dealing with a secondary activity.[24]

ii. Descartes has confused spontaneous doubt, which is a consciousness, with methodological doubt, which is an act. When we catch a glimpse of an object, there may be a doubting consciousness of the object as uncertain. But Descartes' cogito has posited this consciousness itself as an object: the Cartesian cogito is not one with the doubting consciousness but has reflected upon it.[25]

On the basis of above observations, Sartre has concluded as follows:

> This cogito is not Descartes doubting: it is Descartes reflecting upon the doubting. "I doubt therefore I am", is really, "I am aware that I doubt; therefore I am". The Cartesian cogito is reflective, and its object is not itself but the original consciousness of doubting. The consciousness which doubted is now reflected on by the cogito but was never itself reflective: its only object is

---

[23] Chalmers, 2002, *Philosophy of Mind*, p. 2.

[24] Sartre, 1984, *Being and Nothingness*, "Translator's Note", p. xi.

[25] Ibid.

> the object which it is conscious of as doubtful. These conclusions lead Sartre to establish the pre-refelctive cogito as the primary consciousness.[26]

For details, see Chapter 4 which deals with consciousness in Jean-Paul Sartre's philosophy of Existentialism.

Vedāntic Interpretation of Descartes's Formula: "I Think Therefore I Am"

According to Vedānta school of Indian philosophy, consciousness is embodied in human being. It becomes self-consciousness because it manifests through the mind. That is why a person is spontaneously conscious of his own existence as "I am". Therefore Descartes' formula has been interpreted by the Vedānta as "I am therefore I think".[27]

SOME SCIENTIFIC FACTS AS SOLUTION OF THE MIND–BODY PROBLEM

The mind–body problem is known as, how some physical particles in brain can cause the mental experiences.[28] This has been rephrased in science as, "is the mental just the physical". In this context, it is observed:

> The explanatory adequacy of physics leads directly to the conclusion that the mental states are physical states (as Lewis points out). Take pain. Pain has physical effects: it can cause you to take aspirin, or hold your hand to your head, for example. According to the explanatory adequacy of physics, physical effects have physical explanations; more precisely; all physical phenomena are in principle ultimately explainable in terms of "fundamental particles or fields governed by a few simple laws, more or less as conceived of in present-day theoretical physics" (Lewis, 1971, p. 169). It follows trivially that the physical effects

---

26 Sartre, 1984, op. cit., p. xi.

27 Swami Satprakashananda, 1965, *Methods of Knowledge*, p. 83.

28 Searle, 2004, op. cit., p. 3.

> of pain are so explainable. Of course, pain is what explains these effects; consequently; pain itself is ultimately completely described and explained in terms of fundamental physics.[29]

The above explanatory adequacy of physics has been denied by Thomas Nagel. This is explained below:

> We have increasing knowledge of a fascinating character about the physical conditions of particular types of conscious states, but these correlations, even if substantially multiplied, do not amount to a general explanatory theory. In order to achieve a real understanding of these matters, we would have to make progress of a fundamental kind with the mind–body problem; progress which constituted a conceptual advance, rather than merely more empirically ascertainable information, however interesting. A theory which succeeded in explaining the relation between behavior, consciousness, and the brain would have to be of a fundamentally different kind from theories about other things. It cannot be generated the application of already existing methods of explanation.[30]

It may, however, be noted that the scientific concept of the mental state as physical one is also known as the materialism. The materialistic philosophy has been started from the ancient Greece. The elementary particles were seen as ultimate indestructible units of matter in the Democritean sense. According to him, "the material atoms alone can account for the whole universe".[31]

Materialism may be justified on the basis of following observations:

i. Modern science admits that "its subject of study is primarily our observation of nature, and not nature itself. The new picture must then inevitably involve mind as well as matter — the mind which perceives and the matter which is

---

[29] Warner and Szubka (eds), 1994, *The Mind–Body Problem*, p. 2.

[30] Ibid., p. 3.

[31] Masih, 2002, *A Critical History of Western Philosophy*, p. 3.

perceived".[32] This shows that perceiving and perceived are one and the same thing because both are the act of human being. In this approach there is no duality between the mind and the matter and hence there is no scope of the mind–body dualism.

ii. It is observed that "the materialists do not recognize anything like the mind–body dualism. They hold that the mind is simply the brain. And hence all processes are physical and none is mental. Thus the materialists try to solve the mind–body problem by doing away with mind and recognizing matter only".[33]

iii. When the energy of the fundamental matter (*prakṛti*) gradually increases, it acquires the form of *caitanya* (consciousness).[34]

The Identity Theory

In the identity theory, the mind is treated as identical to brain. According to a few neuroscientists, "the mind arises from the integrated activity of large population of neurons distributed along multiple brain regions. It is also proposed that each neuron in the neuron system is independently conscious".[35] This identity theory does not seem to be appropriate mainly because of the following reasons.

i. The mind is subjective and personal, and for this reason the mind and the self cannot be reduced to the brain.[36] The similar observation in different words has been made by Searle as mentioned earlier.

ii. There is no one place in the brain at which the images

[32] Swami Ranganathananda, 2001, *The Message of the Upanishads*, p. 332.

[33] Panda, 2013, *Mind and Supermind*, vol. II, pp. 354-55.

[34] Tilak, 2000, *Gita-Rahasya*, p. 218.

[35] Bhattacharya, 2009, "Molecules that Are Involved in Cellular Consciousness", p. 268.

[36] Feinberg, 2001, op. cit., p. 139.

physically come together. Rather, the two images create a mental condition where their meanings are conjointly represented in awareness to produce a higher level of meaning.[37]

Nested Hierarchy of Brain

The brain functions in a nested hierarchy. So is the case with all biological systems. Therefore, "the proper model for the integration of the mind and brain is that of a nested hierarchy".[38] Now the question is that "how is the mental representation of a face unified in awareness if so many areas of the brain are involved in its manifestation? The convergence of neural pathways makes possible cell so specific that it will only fire to face. This process might lead to think that a single "grandmother" cell, at the top of perceptual hierarchy, embodies the representation of an entire face in consciousness."[39] In this nested hierarchy, "higher brain regions purposely control lower regions is one of the cornerstones of modern neurological thought".[40] This is explained below:

> The nervous system evolved from a simple reflexes that could be found at the lowest hierarchical levels of the nervous system to voluntary forms of action that are produced by the highest cortical levels of the brain. Jackson's hierarchical nervous system views higher cortical regions as controlling and suppressing lower levels. What appears at the top of a Jacksonian action is not a pontifical cell. Jackson had no image of a "ghost in the machine" controlling lower levels of the nervous system. For Jackson, it was purposeful action, or what Jackson referred to as voluntary (as opposed to automatic) behavior that sits at the highest levels of the nervous system. Voluntary behaviors were the most complex, most specialized, least automatic, involved the

---

[37] Feinberg, 2001, op. cit., p. 131.

[38] Ibid., p. 129.

[39] Ibid.

[40] Ibid., p. 135.

> greatest degree of consciousness, and had the greatest degree of independence from other movements. Voluntary action was also the most conscious form of action. It was voluntary or purposeful action that constrains the lower elements in the motor hierarchy, not a single cell or brain region.[41]

It is further observed that "in the nested hierarchy of an organism, all its parts — the cell, tissues, organs — are alive, and the life of the parts is what makes the entire thing alive".[42]

The above observations of Feinberg get diluted when he has agreed to Searle's finding that "mind cannot be reduced to the brain".[43]

That apart, the fact, however, remains that the quantum physics provides the solution to the mind-body problem. This is based on the new concept of matter as wholeness and implicate order profounded by David Bohm.

David Bohm's Concept of Matter

MATTER: WHOLENESS AND IMPLICATE ORDER

Bohm's contribution in developing a new theory of the relation between consciousness and matter in a scientific manner is the most exciting.[44] However, it has been observed:

> In a discussion of the "wave function of the universe", the implicate and generative order of the whole is involved. Out of this whole emerge sub-wholes (including observers), which themselves can be organized into wider context, and these in turn are further organized until the total universe is encompassed in this way.[45]

---

[41] Feinberg, 2001, op. cit., p. 135.

[42] Ibid., p. 151.

[43] Ibid., p. 141.

[44] Capra, 1989, *The Tao of Physics*, p. 352.

[45] Bohm and Peat, 1987, *Science, Order and Creativity*, p. 196.

An attempt has recently been made to examine the Bohm's contribution in establishing the relationship between consciousness and matter in a logical framework. This is evident from the following observation:

> Matter as a whole can be understood in terms of the notion that the implicate order is the immedīate and primary actuality (while explicate order can be derived as a particular, distinguished case of the implicate order) . . . . If matter and consciousness could in this way be understood together, in terms of the same general notion of order, the way would be opened to comprehending their relationship on the basis of some common ground. Thus, we could come to the germ of a new notion of unbroken wholeness, in which consciousness is no longer to be fundamentally separated from the matter. David Bohm points out that if all actions are in the form of discrete quanta, the interactions between entities (e.g. electrons) constitute a single structure of indivisible links, so that the entire universe has to be thought of as an unbroken whole. . . . Eventually Bohm points out that matter and consciousness are manifestations of implicate order, which enfolds all that which is. We may remark that this is strikingly similar to the Vedāntic notion, in the light of which a contradiction between the mind and the body is resolved.[46]

What Is Order

Order has been defined by Bohm in a very broad sense. "Whatever we do pre-supposes some kind of order".[47] However, order may be experienced in a number of different ways. For instance,

> There is the order of number, of points on a line, of space and time, of the movement of a particle through space, and of the functioning of a machine. But order need not be only mechanical or restricted to inanimate systems.[48]

---

[46] Joshi, 2006, "Life, Mind and Consciousness", pp. 25-26.

[47] Bohm and Peat, 1987, op. cit., p. 111.

[48] Ibid.

Interconnection between Consciousness and Matter

The existence of an electron particle as well as electron wave is complementary in the quantum field theory of physics. This paves the way to find out an essential link between consciousness and the primary field. It may be noted that "the fundamental realities of the primary field and consciousness are inseparable aspects of the same underlying process".[49] It has been observed:

> David Bohm has named this underlying process the implicate order. Basil Hiley suggests: Mind and matter are but different projections from this deeper implicate order, where such a division does not exist. He also emphasizes that "the implicate order is not some woolly metaphysical construction, it is a precise description of the underlying process", which is supported by credible mathematical analysis.[50]

It is reassuringly to be told that the implicate order provides the solution to the mind–body problem. This is mainly because "the quantum theory implies certain quality of wholeness in the sense that a system cannot be dealt with properly as a set of separate parts".[51] The connection of the mind and the body is explained in the following words:

> In the implicate order we have to say that mind enfolds matter in general and therefore the body in particular. Similarly, the body enfolds not only mind but also in some sense the entire material universe.[52]

This in a way has solved the mind–body problem.

---

[49] Bhaumik, 2005, *Code Name God*, p. 176.

[50] Ibid.

[51] Bohm and Peat, 1987, op. cit., p. 134.

[52] Bohm, 2012, *Wholeness and the Implicate Order*, p. 265.

1

Explanatory Gap in Phenomenal Consciousness
Solution in East–West Perspective

Introduction

THERE is explanatory gap in the phenomenal consciousness dealt in the Western philosophy. In this chapter, an attempt has been made to explain phenomenal consciousness through access consciousness. Phenomenal consciousness and access consciousness are treated as two different phenomena. The fact, however, is that phenomenal consciousness happens to be merely the manifestation of access consciousness, which is accessible to each and every one of us. The field of access consciousness is embodied in human being according to Advaita Vedānta school of Indian philosophy. In Western philosophy it may be referred as representational consciousness.

Phenomenal consciousness is treated as the central sort of consciousness, mainly because it has experiential properties of sensation, perceptions, thoughts, wants and emotions.[1] However, phenomenal consciousness has been distinguished from access consciousness (access to information), self-consciousness (representation of oneself) and monitoring consciousness (representation of one's own mental states).[2] These notions of consciousness are important, but phenomenal consciousness is

---

[1] Block, 2002, "Concepts of Consciousness", p. 206.

[2] Chalmers, 2002, *Philosophy of Mind*, p. 197.

by far most puzzling, mainly because in science and philosophy, explanations are required in objective terms, whereas consciousness happens to be subjective by its nature.[3] Phenomenal consciousness is also different from intentional content.[4]

Further, phenomenal consciousness is representational. Its properties are distinct from any cognitive, intentional or functional property.[5] There is explanatory gap in phenomenal consciousness because it contrasts with understanding of the scientific basis of cognition.[6] Block has, however, mentioned the following differences between phenomenal consciousness and access consciousness:

i. Phenomenal conscious content is phenomenal, whereas as access consciousness is representational.[7]

ii. Phenomenal consciousness is not a functional notion, whereas access consciousness is representative in its content.[8]

iii. The paradigm phenomenal conscious states are sensations, whereas the paradigm access conscious states are "propositional attitude" states like thoughts, beliefs and desires, states with representational content.[9]

Despite the above differences, it is stated that both phenomenal consciousness and access consciousness interact.[10] How they interact has not been explained. It has also been stated that phenomenal consciousness takes place without access consciousness in some situations. Similarly access consciousness also takes place without

---

[3] Chalmers, 2002, op. cit., p. 197.

[4] Block, 2002, op. cit., p. 206.

[5] Ibid., p. 207.

[6] Ibid.

[7] Ibid., p. 208.

[8] Ibid., p. 209.

[9] Ibid.

[10] Ibid.

phenomenal consciousness.[11]

That apart, the fact remains that in the same book, Rosenthal has categorically stated that "phenomenal consciousness cannot occur without access consciousness".[12] The importance of access consciousness has, however, been reassured by Sartre's observation:

> The problems of the relations between I and consciousness are thus existential problems. Husserl takes up Kant's transcendental consciousness and grasps it by means of the epoché. But this consciousness is no longer a set of logical conditions, but an absolute fact. It is no longer a *de jure* hypothesis, an unconscious that floats between real and ideal realms. It is real consciousness, accessible to each and every one of us, one we have performed the "reduction". The fact remains that it is indeed this transcendental consciousness that constitutes our empirical consciousness, consciousness "in the world", consciousness with a psychical and psycho-physical me. As far as I am concerned, I am quite happy to believe in the existence of a constitutive consciousness.[13]

The epoché, the phenomenological reduction, is the bracketing of the natural attitude, always imbued as it is with a spontaneous realism.[14] Three things emerge from the above observations:

i. Phenomenal consciousness cannot occur without access consciousness,
ii. access consciousness is real one, accessible to each and every one of us, and
iii. transcendental consciousness constitutes our empirical consciousness.

If Block would have taken the above observations into consideration, he would have easily explained the phenomenal

[11] Block, 2002, op. cit., pp. 211-13.

[12] Rosenthal, 2002, "Explaining Consciousness", p. 412.

[13] Sartre, 2012, *The Transcendence of the Ego*, p. 4.

[14] Ibid., p. 55.

consciousness.

It may be noted that self-consciousness itself happens to be the self-identity of human being. This self-consciousness, when manifests or reflects, becomes phenomenal consciousness or reflective consciousness. The source of both phenomenal consciousness and reflective consciousness is self-consciousness which is embodied in human being. Phenomenal consciousness is an objectified state of my self-consciousness according to Vedānta school of Indian philosophy. Therefore, it may be stated that unless the pathway of reflection of self-consciousness is taken into consideration, it is, indeed, difficult to explain phenomenal consciousness as mentioned by Block.

Now let us see how Rosenthal has explained phenomenal consciousness through higher-order thought (HOT).

Higher-Order Thought as Explanation of Phenomenal Consciousness

HOT explains satisfactorily with the phenomenon of state consciousness, even for the special case of sensory states.[15] This is evident from the fact that, "we are conscious of those states by having thoughts about them. And, because these thoughts are about other mental states, we can call them higher-order thoughts (HOTs)."[16] It has been, further, explained in the following observations:

1. HOT would be conscious only when one has a third-order thought about it, and we can assume that such third-order thoughts are rare.[17]
2. The HOT hypothesis explains awareness of the self not perceptually, but by appeal to our having thoughts about the

[15] Rosenthal, 2002, op. cit., p. 417.

[16] Rosenthal, 2005, *Consciousness and Mind*, p. 4.

[17] Ibid., p. 8.

self. . . . HOTs are seldom conscious, but when they are, we have a reflective, introspective awareness of the self. HOTs make us conscious not only of our mental states, but also of the self that is in those states.[18]

3. The mental state itself causes that higher-order thought to occur.[19]
4. Although discussions of consciousness often make metaphorical appeal to the so-called inner sense, no such sense actually exists.[20]
5. Higher-order thought . . . allows a ready distinction between a mental state's being introspectively and non-introspectively conscious. Mental states are introspectively conscious if the relevant higher-order thought is itself a conscious thought.[21]
6. The HOT model explains the difference between mental phenomena that are conscious and those which are not. On their own, thoughts, perceptions and feelings are not conscious. Their sometimes being conscious consists in their being accompanied in those cases by suitable HOTs about them. By "suitable", I mean that whenever the HOT is conscious, it seems spontaneous, and therefore, unmediated. Those HOTs make us conscious of our conscious thoughts, feelings and perceptions, though typically the HOTs are not themselves conscious.[22]
7. The only other way we are conscious of things is having thoughts about them as being present. So, that must be how we are aware of conscious states: a state is conscious if one has a HOT about that state. We seem to be conscious of our

---

[18] Rosenthal, 2005, op. cit., p. 16.

[19] Ibid., p. 25.

[20] Ibid., p. 43.

[21] Ibid., p. 130.

[22] Ibid., p. 273.

conscious states in a direct unmediated way. We can capture that intuitive immediacy by stipulating that HOTs seem to one to rely on no inference of which one is conscious. We are seldom aware of any such HOTs. But we can explain that by supposing that it's rare that HOTs are accompanied by third-order thoughts, and hence rare that HOTs are, themselves, conscious.[23]

8. The atomistic character of this model, however, may seem to prevent it from being able to explain our sense of the unity of consciousness. If each conscious state owes its consciousness to a distinct HOT, how could we come to have a sense of such unity? Why would all our conscious states seem belong to a single, unified self?[24]
9. In the case of unity, Rosenthal has discussed Kant's concept of transcendental unity of self-consciousness (B-132). In this context, it is observed that it is unclear how any such transcendental posit could explain the appearance of conscious mental unity, since that appearance is itself an empirical occurrence.[25]
10. Kant's observation about the dispersed character of empirical consciousness suggests that no empirical account can help explain such actual unity.[26]
11. The HOT model suffices to explain such unity . . . we can regard the thought as in effect characterizing that referent as the individual who thinks that very thought. Each first-person thought thus disposes us to have another thought that identifies the self as the thinker of that first-person thought. . . . Every HOT characterizes the self it refers to

---

[23] Rosenthal, 2005, op. cit., p. 297.

[24] Ibid., pp. 297-98.

[25] Ibid., p. 298.

[26] Ibid.

> solely as the bearer of target states and, in effect, as the thinker of the HOT itself. Nothing in that characterization implies that this bearer is the same from one HOT to the next. But there is also nothing to distinguish one bearer from another. And our seeming to be aware in a direct and unmediated way of the self each HOT refers to tilts things towards apparent unity. Since we seem to be directly aware of the self in each case, it seems subjectively as thought there is a single self to which all one's HOT refer, a single bearer for all conscious states. . . . This helps explain why our sense of unity seems to go hand in hand with our ability to engage in introspective consciousness. . . . Introspective consciousness results in a sense of one's conscious states as all unified in a single conscious subject. . . . One cannot find a self when one seeks it perceptively. The HOT model, by contrast, provides an informative explanation of the way we do seem to be introspectively conscious of the self.[27]

Critical Assessment

It is, indeed, difficult to understand how HOT can explain the phenomenal consciousness? This is mainly because thought happens to be the object of consciousness. This is explained as:

> The actual thought that results is always in terms of the senses, no matter how abstract that thought may be or by what intuition it may have been arrived at. As an example, man is used in the title of this book to denote the characteristics of the human state. But no sooner is the word apprehended than some kind of visual representation appears, however, vaguely, before the mind's eye. Similarly, all abstract notions, whether they refer to qualities, numbers, relations or concepts, require the support of some object of sensory perception, even if it be only a symbol such as cipher or a sound. Abstract thoughts and generalizations are, therefore, the objects of consciousness. As such they are quite

[27] Rosenthal, 2005, op. cit., pp. 299-301.

distinct from introversion.[28]

The above observation may be reassured by the fact that thought is the objective side of consciousness, whereas the self of human being is known as self-consciousness which happens to subjective side of consciousness. Therefore, it may be said that even HOT cannot appropriately explain phenomenal consciousness.

According to Sartre, consciousness can be the source of consciousness.[29] If this view is accepted, phenomenal consciousness can be explained either by access consciousness or self-consciousness. It may be noted that Rosenthal has observed that phenomenal consciousness cannot occur without access consciousness as mentioned earlier. In the same paper, Rosenthal has also stated that the HOT explains phenomenal consciousness. This view is not consistent with earlier view in the sense that HOT is objective side of consciousness whereas access consciousness may be representing the subjective side of consciousness.

According to Rosenthal, HOTs have also the atomistic character. Its implication is quite important for both: thought process and the atom. This is explained below:

> When an atom makes a transition, or a 'jump' from one stationery state to another, the actual process cannot be visualized or imagined. There is no intermediate stages. We cannot breakdown into its components. The entire process of transition from one state to another is non-visualizable, unanalyzable, unity. It is indivisible. Its parts cannot even be imagined. It is a "quantum jump" as we call it. The interesting thing is that there is an analogous situation for thought processes. As we "think" — in any sequence of thoughts — there is always, a sudden, discontinuous jump from one thought to the next. We are not aware at all of any intermediate stages. If we were so aware, no thinking would be possible. There would be an almost infinite sequence of

[28] Levy, 2004, *The Nature of Man According to the Vedānta*, p. 29.

[29] Sartre, 2012, op. cit., p. 15.

> "sub-thoughts" between two thoughts, like an infinity of points between the two ends of a line. Quantum jumps for thought appear to be as much a necessity for the conscious self as these are for the atom.[30]

Kant's Philosophy

SOUL–BODY DUALISM

It is stated that, "I, as thinking, am an object of the internal sense, and am called soul. That which is an object of the external senses is called body".[31] This is generally referred to as body–mind problem. Kant does not seem to provide any specific solution to the mind–body problem. However, thinking is defined in terms of consciousness as follows:

> Consciousness is so constituted that, inasmuch as the thinking subject is at the same time its own object, it cannot divide itself — although it can divide its inhering determinations. For every object in relation to itself is absolute unity.[32]

The Concept of "I Think"

This is explained below:

> The "I think" must accompany all my representations, for otherwise something would be represented in me which could not be thought; in other words, the representation would either be impossible, or at least be, in relation to me, nothing. That representation which can be given previously to all thought is called intuition. All the diversity or manifold content of intution, has, therefore, a necessary relation to the "I think", in the subject in which this diversity is found. But this representation, "I think", is an act of spontaneity; that is to say, it cannot be regarded as belonging to mere sensibility. I call it pure apperception, in order to distinguish it from empirical; or primitive apperception,

---

[30] Kothari, 2002, "Atom and Self", p. 298.

[31] Kant, 1950, *The Critique of Pure Reason*, p. 234.

[32] Ibid., p. 271.

> because it is self-consciousness which, whilst it gives birth to the representation "I think", must necessarily be capable of accompanying all our representations. It is in all acts of consciousness one and the same, and unaccompanied by it, no representation can exist for me. The unity of this apperception I call the transcendental unity of self-consciousness, in order to indicate the possibility of a priori cognition arising from it. For the manifold representations which are given in an intuition would not all of them be my representations, if they did not all belong to one self-consciousness.[33]

Transcendental Unity of Self-consciousness

The transcendental unity of self-consciousness has been introduced by Kant, in the second edition of *The Critique of Pure Reason* evident in the following observation:

> As a self-consciousness that is devoid of material content, Kant describes this original unity as "pure" and original apperception (B132); as the condition of the possibility of empirical self-consciousness he also calls it transcendental apperception (A107) in the first edition, and in the second edition the transcendental unity of self-consciousness (B132) or more simply transcendental self-consciousness. The empirical subject which accompanies different representations, judging now this object and now that is in itself diverse. This subject lacks unity in its constant change. It only acquires the identity of the subject through a pre-empirical contribution that does not change, through that combining of representations in one consciousness whereby "I represent to myself the identity of the consciousness throughout these representations" (B133). This representation is a synthetic unity of self-consciousness in so far as it accomplishes such combination, it is an original unity of self-consciousness.[34]

In the above observation, the transcendental unity of self-consciousness has been mixed up by the notions of subjective and

[33] Kant, 1950, op. cit., p. 96.

[34] Hoffe, 2010, *Kant's Ctitique of Pure Reason*, p. 156.

objective. This is explained below:

> The empirical self-consciousness or what he calls empirical apperception or inner sense is subjective, but the transcendent unity of self-consciousness, which is also the synthetic unity of self-consciousness is called objective. It is called objective because of its transcendental role, intersubjective, sameness in all, and also in the sense of being responsible for the concept of object. We can note how the notions of "subjective" and "objective" are being mixed up in Kant.[35]

The subjective and the objective notions of transcendental unity of self-consciousness have been reconciled by Kant. Hoffe says:

> Kant concludes part proof II and draws the relevant conclusion (Section 26): "the categories are conditions of the possibility of experience, and are therefore valid a priori for all objects of experience" (B 161). The categories are thus capable of "prescribing, as it were, the law to nature" (B 159). Given the thoroughgoing correlation between subjectivity and objectivity, we cannot explain the transcendental structures of subjectivity without simultaneously grasping the pre-empirical features of objectivity. Nor, for the same reason, can we understand the "deduction" without simultaneously considering the lawfulness of nature that is implicit in the categories, the pre-empirical presuppositions of the synthetic unity of apperception when he finally completes the actual empirical laws of nature. It is only to be expected, therefore, that Kant returns to the question of the "deduction" in the chapter on "The System of All Principles of Pure Understanding". The transcendental "I think" is at once the unity of self-consciousness and the unity of nature, and thus both subjectivity and objectivity in one.[36]

It is, however, stated that, "unity of consciousness and unity of

---

[35] Chatterjee et al., 2014, *J.N. Mohanty Lectures on Kant's Critique of Pure Reason*, p. 185.

[36] Hoffe, 2010, op. cit., p. 161.

object are one and the same thing".[37] This has been shown by example as follows:

> If in counting, I forget that the units, which now hover before me, have been added to one another in succession. I should never know that a total is being produced through this successive addition of unit, and so would remain ignorant of the number. For the concept of number is nothing but the consciousness of this unity of synthesis.[38] This is the Kantian move. A number is generated by synthesis a priori synthesis, while counting we are not merely going from one to another, but we are adding the succeeding one to the preceding one. There are three things here. Unity = concept of unity = consciousness of synthesis.[39]

In the above unity three things are not different but they are one. It is known as the transcendental unity of self-consciousness. This unity is treated by Searle as a unified structure of consciousness which comes to us.[40]

VEDĀNTIC INTERPRETATION OF TRANSCENDENTAL UNITY OF SELF-CONSCIOUSNESS

Consciousness at transcendental becomes the Ultimate Reality at ontological or metaphysical principle.[41] It is further stated that, "knowledge of transcendental consciousness enables to face the mystery of death. The survival of consciousness after death is the greatest challenge to science and the greatest support to religion".[42]

However, the transcendental unity of self-consciousness seems to be like *Ātman* (Absolute Reality) of Indian philosophy. It is known, "as *astitva-jñāna* of *Brahman*, that is, the awareness that *Brahman*

---

[37] Chatterjee et al., 2014, op. cit., p. 162.

[38] Ibid.

[39] Ibid.

[40] Searle, 2004, *Mind: A Brief Introduction*, p. 95.

[41] Swami Bhajananda, 2009, "Knowledge and Consciousness", p. 92.

[42] Ibid., p. 99.

exists. It does not need any proof: It is self evident."[43] When ure Consciousness (Absolute Reality) descends in human being, it becomes self-consciousness, which is referred to as witness self (*sākṣī*). It illumines the mental states: knowledge, ignorance, pain, etc. "The mental states are immediately cognized because of their presence to the witness self."[44]

NOUMENON

It may be noted that the term noumenon has been used by Kant in both ways: negative and positive. If the object is not our sensuous intuition, noumenon is used in the negative sense.[45] "But if we understand by it an object of a non-sensuous intuition, we in this case assume a peculiar mode of intuition, an intellectual intuition, to wit, which does not, however, belong to us, of the very possibility of which we have no notion — and this a noumenon in the positive sense".[46] It has also been mentioned by Kant that, "the doctrine of sensibility is also the doctrine of noumena in the negative sense, that is, of things which the understanding is obliged to cogitate apart from any relation to mode of intuition, consequently not as mere phenomena but as the things in themselves".[47] However, according to Kant, the possibility of noumena is quite incomprehensible and beyond the sphere of phenomena, all is for us a mere void.[48] What emerges is that noumena is empty and limiting concept and used in the negative sense by Kant.

VEDĀNTIC INTERPRETATION OF NOUMENA

The manifestation of consciousness is, however, treated as the

---

[43] Swami Bhajananda, 2009, op. cit., p. 93.

[44] Swami Satprakashananda, 2001, *Methods of Knowledge*, p. 91.

[45] Kant, 1950, op. cit., p. 186.

[46] Ibid., pp. 186-87.

[47] Ibid., p. 187.

[48] Ibid., p. 188.

objective aspect of the subjective awareness.[49] It may be noted that, "noumenon being pure subjective, cannot see itself as noumenon. The phenomenal manifestation, therefore, is not something from outside, projected by the noumenon, but is an objectivization as manifestation on and within itself".[50] It shows that the essential identity between noumenon and phenomena is innate.

SARTRE'S INTERPRETATION OF NOUMENA

It is observed that "a consciousness which would be behind its perceptible manifestations as the noumenon is behind the Kantian *Empfindung*".[51]

The above interpretations of Kant's philosophy indicate that phenomenal consciousness may be easily explained through the transcendental unity of self-consciousness.

Pratyabhijñā (Recognition) School of Kashmir Śaivism

In *pratyabhijñā*, recognition is defined as:

> Recognition, however, must not be identified either with memory (*smṛti*) or with perceptual cognition (*pratykṣa-jñāna*). It is, rather, the combination of both. Memory is given rise due to the activation of the subliminal impressions (*saṁskāras*). Although through perception an object may be cognized as well as perceived, but it is never recognized. In the event of recognition what happens is that the mental impression goes invariably along with the direct perception of the object. The uniqueness of recognition lies in the fact that the object that is being cognized is easily identified with the object that has previously been known. Thus, recognition is characterized by an intuitive awareness with regard to the identity of the substance

---

[49] Balsekar, 1999, *Pointers from Nisargadatta Maharaj*, p. 225.

[50] Ibid., p. 226.

[51] Sartre, 1984, *Being and Nothingness*, p. 340.

that persists through its two states.[52]

TWO ASPECTS OF CONSCIOUSNESS: LIGHT AND AWARENESS

Absolute consciousness as the unchanging ontological ground of all appearance is known as *prakāśa.* "As the creative awareness of its own Being, the absolute is called *vimarśa. Prakāśa* and *vimarśa* — the Divine Light of consciousness and the reflective awareness, this light has its own nature — together constitute the all-embracing fullness (*pūrṇatā*) of consciousness."[53]

LIGHT OF CONSCIOUSNESS (PRAKĀŚA)

Prakāśa being the pure luminosity (*bhāna*) is like pure consciousness (*Ātman*) of Vedānta. It is treated as the absolute reality. In its light, "everything appears there according to its own specific nature (*svabhāva*). . . . The universe is nothing but the shining of the light within itself. It is the radiant vibration (*sphuratā*) of this light, the state (*avasthāna*) in which consciousness manifest."[54] It is further observed that "everything is made manifest by the light of consciousness and, as such, attains its true being by realizing its unity with all".[55] However, this concept of absolute reality as "light and its manifestations as reflections have led us to consider its universal power apparent through its recurring pulsations of activity. This same power generates both forms within itself and is conscious of them. Therefore, this, the absolute's power of self awareness, to which we now turn, is also spanda, its vibration."[56]

SELF-AWARENESS AND CONSCIOUSNESS

The act of reflective awareness is known as *vimarśa.* The world is

---

52 M.L. Pandit, 2012, *The Philosophical and Practical Aspects of Kashmir Śaivism,* p. 78.

53 Dyczkowski, 2006, *The Doctrine of Vibration,* p. 59.

54 Ibid., p. 60.

55 Torella and Bäumer, 2016, *Utpaladeva,* p. 361.

56 Dyczkowski, 2006, op. cit., p. 68.

derived from the root *mrs* which means to touch, feel, understand, perceive, reflect or examine. "Thus, *vimarśa* is the power of consciousness by virtue of which it can understand or perceive itself, feel, reflect on and examine the events that occur within it. . . . This ability to reflect on it on itself is inherent in the very nature of the light of consciousness: indeed it is the most specific characteristic."[57]

The *vimarśa* seems to have two aspects:

i. Internal — This is the act of awareness when the light of consciousness rests in itself alone. It is the pure awareness of "I" (*ahaṁvimarśa*), devoid of all thought constructs (*nirvikalpa*), said to be total freedom and unsullied wonder.[58]

ii. External — This aspect corresponds to the act of reflection directed away from the subject to the object he perceives as separate from himself. Reality then becomes accessible to discursive representation (*vikalpa*) and amenable to empirical definition.[59]

The relationship between internal and external *vimarśa* is explained below:

> Awareness serves to relate objectivity (external) and subjectivity (internal) in such a way that the object ultimately comes to rest in the self-awareness of the subject. In reality, reflective awareness is always awareness of "I" (*ahaṁvimarśā*): it never objectivises even when, in the form of the awareness of "this" (*idamvimarśā*), it reflects upon the object. The experience we have of things existing outside consciousness is due to lack of self-awareness. The awareness is never out there; it is registered and known within the subject. All forms of awareness come to rest in the subject. Just as every drop of water comes to rest in the ocean, so all acts and cognitions [come to rest] in the Great Lord, the ocean

---

[57] Dyczkowski, 2006, op. cit., p. 69.

[58] Ibid., p. 70.

[59] Ibid.

> of consciousness. . . . Individual and universal consciousness are one. The same processes operate in both: the only difference between them is that in the case of individual consciousness these processes are restricted or limited (*saṁkucita*) representations of the maximally expended (*vikāsita*) operation of universal consciousness. The activity of the mind is that of consciousness itself, or to be more precise, of its reflective awareness, the power of *spanda*.[60]

Reflective awareness (*vimarśa*) is characterized as action, whereas the light (*prakāśa*) is knowledge (*jñāna*) or passive being. In other words, awareness is the creative act of making reality known, while the light is the actuality of its being known. The latter without the former would be an inactive principle, a state of pure potential that could never actualize into an act of awareness. From point of view two aspects of awareness are:[61]

(i) *Karma vimarśa* – When the act of awareness is directed externally and coincides with the unfolding (*vikāsa*) of the extension of the universe (*prapañca*) out of the absolute.[62]

(ii) *Kriyā vimarśa* —When this activity is still unlimited and infinite, completely internalized within the absolute as its agency (*kartṛtva*), undistributed by any goal of action (*kārya*) as the pure vibration or stir (*saṁrambha*) of consciousness.[63]

The relation between: *karma vimarśa* and *kriyā vimarśa* is explained as:

> Knowledge and action together constitute the basis of daily life and the life of all living beings. One is never without the other: they function hand in hand. At the universal level, the power of action evolves forms out of the pleroma of consciousness, while the power of knowledge makes them manifest. On the

[60] Dyczkowski, 2006, op. cit., p. 71.

[61] Ibid., p. 72.

[62] Ibid.

[63] Ibid.

> individual level, they represent the objective and subjective poles of all sentient activity. As the inner awareness that "I am" (*ahaṁ*), knowledge is the stable referent of all actions. It persists undivided throughout all action, however, diverse.[64]

From the above observations, it is evident that reflective consciousness (reflective awareness) or phenomenal consciousness are the manifestation of pure consciousness or pure ego. Therefore, the former is explained by the latter. This shows that there is no explanatory gap in reflective consciousness or phenomenal consciousness in the philosophy of Pratyabhijñā (Recognition) of Kashmir Śaivism.

[64] Dyczkowski, 2006, op. cit., p. 72.

2

Mind and Consciousness in East–West Perspective

Introduction

The essence of mind is consciousness, according to Descartes. This has been the starting point for the Western philosophy in the modern era. The mind has been identified with consciousness in the Western philosophy. It is stated that, "Consciousness is the only distinctive characteristic of mind".[1] This is reassured by the two fundamental aspects of mind; consciousness and intentionality.[2] On the basis of these observations an inference has been drawn that "in Western thought, consciousness is identified with the mind and the mind is identified with the brain".[3] However, there is an exception also in the Western thought under which the distinction has been made between the mind and the consciousness. Sir William Hamilton Bart has defined mind and consciousness precisely with clarity. The mind being an act of knowledge is expressed by the formula: I know, whereas an act of consciousness is known by the formula, I know that I know.[4]

Bart has also compared consciousness with an internal light, "by means of which and which alone what passes in the mind

---

[1] Block et al. (eds), 2002, *The Nature of Consciousness*, p. 23.

[2] Ibid., p. 22.

[3] Swami Bhajanananda, 2009, "Knowledge and Consciousness", p. 53.

[4] Bart, 1995, *Philosophy of Knowledge*, vol. I, p. 193.

is rendered visible".[5] This shows that the mind becomes the object of consciousness, which is fairly comparable to Vedāntic concept of mind, treated as an instrument for the manifestation of consciousness. Since the mind becomes an object of consciousness, Vedānta school of Indian philosophy has defined the mind as insentient (*jaḍa*). This extreme position is mainly due to definitional problem in the sense that all objects of consciousness are treated as insentient (*jaḍa*). The fact, however, is that in Vedānta, *cit* is consciousness. "Mind is consciousness plus unconscious, the intermingled consciousness — unconsciousness which we see in all finite being."[6]

In view of the above observations, the mind and consciousness according to Bart and Vedānta are presented here. This may provide a better understanding in a cross-cultural context.

Western Philosophy

VIEWS OF SIR WILLIAM HAMILTON BART LECTURES ON METAPHYSICS

According to Bart, philosophy is only a systematic evolution of the contents of consciousness. This is mainly because there is no any other ground higher than consciousness. Therefore, one has to invalidate the facts of consciousness on the ground of consciousness itself.[7] In this context, let us see how the mind being a self-knowing principle is explained by Bart.

Mind

The etymology of the mind is obscure and doubtful; "perhaps, indeed, none of the attempts to trace it to its origin is successful".[8] Its root seems to be "lost in the European languages of Scytho-Indian origin, is probably preserved in the Sanskrit *mena, to know*

---

[5] Bart, 1995, op. cit., vol. I, p. 183.

[6] Woodroffe, 2001, *The World as Power*, p. 111.

[7] Bart, 1995, op. cit., vol. I, p. 277.

[8] Ibid., p. 156.

or *understand*".[9] This is explained below:

> Mind, therefore, is to be understood as the subject of the various internal phenomena of which we are conscious, or that subject of which consciousness is the general phenomenon. Consciousness is, in fact, to the mind what extension is to the matter or body. Though both are phenomena, yet both are essential qualities: for we can neither conceive mind without consciousness nor body with extension. Mind can be defined only — *a posteriori* — that is, only from its manifestations. What it is in itself, that is, apart from its manifestations, we philosophically know nothing, and, accordingly, what we mean by mind is simply *that which perceives, thinks, feels, wills, desires*, etc.[10]

The mental phenomena, have, however, been categorized mainly under three groups:

i. cognitive aspect is concerned with knowing,
ii. exertive or affective aspect refers to feeling, pleasure or pain, and
iii. conative aspect is concerned with willing desiring.

These phenomena of mind are not working independently to each other. They work in mutual combination. Such classification of the mental phenomena or of the phenomena of which we are conscious. But these primary classes are, "all included under one universal phenomenon — the phenomenon of consciousness — it follows that consciousness must form the first object of our consideration".[11]

It is further observed that "consciousness lies at the root of all knowledge. Consciousness is itself the one highest source of all comprehensibility and illustration".[12] Consciousness necessarily

---

[9] Bart, 1995, op. cit., vol. I, p. 156.

[10] Ibid., pp. 156-57.

[11] Ibid., p. 189.

[12] Ibid., p. 191.

involves three things: "(i) A recognizing or known subject; (ii) A recognized or known modification; and (iii) A recognition or knowledge by the subject of the modification".[13] Now let us examine how consciousness is defined.

It is important to know what an act consciousness denotes. These acts are quite elementary. But they happen to be the basic conditions of all knowledge. This is explained by Bart as follows.

CONSCIOUSNESS

What act denotes consciousness is explained as:

> You are all familiar with the thing, it is easy to enable you to connect the thing with word, I know — I desire — I feel. What is it that is common to all these? *Knowing* and *desiring* and *feeling* are not the same and may be distinguished. But they all agree in one fundamental condition. Can I know without knowing that I know? Can I desire without knowing that I desire? Can I feel without knowing that I feel? This is impossible. Now this knowing that I know or desire or feel — this common condition of self-knowledge is precisely what is denominated consciousness.[14]

It may be stated that since consciousness comprises within the whole phenomena of mind, "the expression of *conscious-subject* is a brief but comprehensive definition of mind itself".[15] However, "the terms *subjective* and *objective* denote the primary distinction in consciousness of *self* and *not-self*".[16] This is explained below:

> A suspension of thought is thus a suspension of my intellectual existence: I am, therefore, essentially a thinking — a conscious being: and my true character is that of an intelligence — an intelligence served by organs. But this thought, this

[13] Bart, 1995, op. cit., vol. I, p. 193.

[14] Ibid., p. 158.

[15] Ibid.

[16] Ibid., p. 160.

> consciousness, is possible only in and through, the consciousness of Self. The Self, the I, is recognized in every act of intelligence, as the subject to which the act belongs. It is I that perceive, I that imagine, I that remember, I that attend, I that compare, I that feel, I that desire, I that will, I that am conscious. The I, indeed, is only manifested in one or other of these special modes: but it is manifested in them all; they are all only the phenomena of the "I".[17]

It is thus, evident that whatever division of the mental phenomena may be adopted, all its members must be within consciousness. But, it may be noted that consciousness itself cannot be divided. Consciousness remains one, "comprehending all the modifications – all the phenomena of the thinking subject".[18]

The most general characteristic of consciousness is the recognition by the thinking subject of its own acts or affecting as mentioned above. On this there is no dispute in the sense that all philosophers are agreed.[19] But the most arduous task is to determine the special conditions of consciousness. According to Bart, there are five special conditions, which are discussed as follows.

Consciousness as Actual Knowledge

Man is able to know that "7 + 9 are = 16, though that equation be not, at the moment, the object of his thought; but we cannot say that he is conscious of this truth unless while actually present to his mind".[20]

Consciousness as Immediate Knowledge

We know the mental representation and this "we do immediately and in itself, and are also said to know the past occurrence, as mediately knowing it through the mental modification which

---

[17] Bart, 1995, op. cit., vol. I, p. 166.

[18] Ibid., p. 183.

[19] Ibid., p. 201.

[20] Ibid., p. 202.

represents it".[21]

Consciousness as Contrast: A Discrimination

We are conscious of what that something is: "that is, distinguish it from what it is not. This discrimination is of different kinds and degrees".[22] It is explained below:

> We are conscious of self only in and by its contradistinction from non-self; and are conscious of not-self only in and by its contradistinction from self. In the second place, there is the discrimination of states or modifications of the internal subject or self from each other.[23] This shows that discrimination is an essential condition of consciousness.

Consciousness as Judgement

A judgement is the mental act involving by which either affirms or denies the other. "This fourth condition is in truth only a necessary consequence of the third — for it is impossible to discriminate without judging — discrimination, or contradistinction, being in fact only the denying of one thing of another."[24]

Consciousness as Memory

It is stated that without memory the mental states cannot be compared or distinguished from each other and referred to self. This is explained thus:

> The notion of the ego or self arises from the recognized permanence and identity of the thinking subject in contrast to the recognized succession and variety of its modifications. But this recognition is possible only through memory. The notion of

[21] Bart, 1995, op. cit., vol. I, p. 202.

[22] Ibid., p. 203.

[23] Ibid.

[24] Ibid., p. 204.

> self is, therefore, the result of memory. But the notion of self is involved in consciousness, so consequently is memory.[25]

However, memory is mediate knowledge of the past. But in philosophical propriety, "it is not a knowledge of the past at all, but a knowledge of the present and a belief of the past. But in whatever terms we may designate the contents of memory, it is manifest that these contents are all within the sphere of consciousness".[26] It may also be stated that "the hypothesis, which postulates consciousness without memory, violates the fundamental laws of our intellectual being".[27]

CONSCIOUSNESS AND ATTENTION

It seems that, "there is no consciousness without attention, without concentration, but that attention is of three degrees or kinds. The first, a mere vital and irresistible act; the second, an act determined by desire, which though involuntary, may be resisted by our will; and the third, an act determined by a deliberate voliation."[28] It is, further, explained as:

> Attention, then, is to consciousness, what the contraction of the pupil is to sight: or to the eye of the mind, what the microscope or telescope is to the bodily eye. The faculty of attention is not, therefore, a special faculty, but merely consciousness acting under the law of limitation to which it is subjected. But whatever be its relations to the special faculties, attention doubles all their efficiency, and affords them a power of which they would otherwise be destitute. It is, in fact, as we are at present constituted, the primary condition of their activity.[29]

---

[25] Bart, 1995, op. cit., vol. I, p. 205.

[26] Ibid., p. 221.

[27] Ibid., p. 369.

[28] Ibid., pp. 247-48.

[29] Ibid., p. 248.

EXPLANATORY GAP IN PHENOMENAL CONSCIOUSNESS AND MIND–BODY PROBLEM

What emerges from the above observations is that when self-consciousness reflects through the sense organs in external perception, it becomes the phenomenal consciousness. While manifesting it also knows the inner modifications. If one treats self-consciousness as described by Bart it may be possible to explain the phenomenal consciousness. It may also solve the problem of the mind–body, provided of course the distinction is made between mind and consciousness, as has been attempted by Bart. But this will happen only when one is interested in looking at other's study and observations. If one loves his own experience and writing, it will be all the more difficult to provide the solution for explanatory gap in phenomenal consciousness and mind–body problem.

Indian Philosophy: Mind and Consciousness in Upaniṣads

MIND

Mind is known as *manas* in the Upaniṣads. "*Manas*, however, is the repository of several functions and characteristics of which *saṁkalpa* is only the most frequently mentioned."[30] These functions may be seen from the following observations:

> Indeed one sees with the mind, one hears with the mind. Desire, conceptualization, doubt . . . all this is mind. Borne along and defiled by the stream of qualities (*guṇas*), unsteady, fickle, bewildered, full of desire, distracted, one comes to conceit. Thinking, "I am he; this is mine", he entangles himself with himself as a bird in a snare. Thus, the person (*puruṣa*), characterized by determination (*adhyavasāya*), conceptualization (*saṁkalpa*) and conceit (*abhimāna*), is bound. The opposite of that is liberated. Therefore stand free of determination, conceptualization and conceit. This is the path to *Brahman*.[31]

[30] Reat, 1990, *Origins of Indian Psychology*, p. 244.

[31] Ibid., p. 246; source: *Maitrī Upaniṣad* VI.30.

The most important qualities of *manas* are conceptualization (*saṁkalpa*), determination (*adhyavasāya*) and conceit (*abhimāna*), as mentioned above. However, *manas* also of two kinds.

> The mind (*manas*), it is said, is of two kinds, pure and impure, impure from contact with desire and pure when freed from desire. By freeing mind from sloth and distraction and making it motionless, he becomes delivered from his mind, then that is the supreme state. . . . Mind, in truth, is the cause of bondage and liberation for mankind; for bondage if it is bound to objects; freedom from objects, that is called liberation.[32]

CONSCIOUSNESS

In the *Bṛhadāraṇyaka Upaniṣad*, the word *prajñānaghana* (verse IV.5.13) and *vijñānaghana* (II.4.12) indicate "mass of consciousness". This may be explained by the fact that *prajñā*'s sphere is deep sleep under which "all (experiences) become unified or undifferentiated, who is verily a mass of consciousness entire, who is full of bliss and who experiences bliss".[33] However, this mass of consciousness is nothing but pure consciousness which is treated as the Absolute Reality referred to as *Brahman* in Indian philosophy. That apart, the fact remains that the relationship between mind and consciousness has not been established in clear terms in the Upaniṣads.

Mind and Consciousness in Advaita Vedānta

MIND

The mind is called *citta* in the *Yogasūtra*, whereas in Vedānta school of Indian philosophy it is called *antaḥkaraṇa* (internal organ). This has four aspects: *manas, buddhi, citta* and *ahaṁkāra*. It may, however, be stated that according to Vedāntic viewpoint, the human mind is creation of consciousness, so as to act as an organ of interconnection

---

[32] Reat, 1990, op. cit., p. 247; *Maitrī Upaniṣad* VI.34.

[33] Swami Nikhilananda, 2000, *The Māṇḍūkya Upaniṣad with Gauḍapāda's Kārikā and Śaṅkara's Commentary*, p. 21.

between the inner and the outer, the individual and the world. This is explained as follows:

> In this scheme of things, while *citta* represents consciousness as narrowed down in its range and *ahaṁkāra* is rooted in the concentricity of consciousness as such, *buddhi* reflects the decisiveness of consciousness operating on the stuff provided by the shifting *manas*. Considered inversely, the sensory datum gathered from outside by *manas* through senses is being processed by *buddhi* owned by *ahaṁkāra* and is finally merging into consciousness through the agency of *citta*. This is how, explains the Vedāntin, consciousness projects itself individually and universally outside as also gets back the projection to itself both ontologically and epistemologically and thus opens out the entire phenomenon of the world along with life in it.[34]

Buddhists have, however, argued that "the existence of internal organ is mere assumption which can neither be proved, nor is capable to account for the fact of several individual experiences".[35] As against this argument, the Vedāntins have stated that "without the assumption of internal organs actual individual cognition, in its positive aspects as well as its limitations, could not be accounted for".[36] This is further explained below:

> As the internal organ, made up of these three parts, is of an exceedingly pure and transparent nature, Consciousness is manifested through it. Consciousness thus manifested indeed is one only, but is, according to the three several parts of the internal organ which manifest it, denoted by three different terms. That part of Consciousness which is particularized by the agent-part of the internal organ is called "knowing subject" (*pramātṛ*); that part which is particularized by the action-part is called "means of knowledge" (*pramāṇa*); and the part particularized by that part of the internal organ which serves for the manifestation of

---

[34] Singh, 2004, *Vedic Vision of Consciousness and Reality*, pp. 74-75.

[35] Thibaut, 1994, *The Vivaraṇaprameya-Saṁgraha of Vidyāraṇya*, p. 146.

[36] Ibid., p. 147.

> the object is called "(right) knowledge" (*pramit*). In this way the "knowing subject", "the means of knowledge" and "knowledge" are clearly distinguished. In all these three, however, the form of the internal organ is the common factor; and as this form consists only in the relation subsisting between the knowing subject and the object known, it becomes possible for people to make use of such expressions as "this is known by me" – wherein all three appear as qualifying one another (this mutual qualification being made possible by the fact that the three have a factor common to them all). . . . What we maintain rather is that Consciousness is the cause of perception insofar as it is manifested by the internal organ. Now there is a different internal organ for each man; how then can you say that our view implies a confusion of the experiences of all men?[37]

However, the existence of the internal organ has been justified by Śaṅkarācārya for the reason that if the internal is not admitted, either there will be the possibility of either constant perception or non-perception.[38]

MIND AND CONSCIOUSNESS

Pure consciousness alone will not give rise to empirical knowledge.[39] But it also has to be recognized that without a reflection of pure consciousness in the mind (which is known as *cidābhāsa* in Vedānta), the mind will not be in a position to gain experience because it is treated as unconscious. But this relationship between pure consciousness and mind may be explained by using the method of co-presence and co-absence (*anvaya-vyatireka*). This in turn suggests that, if pure consciousness exists, the entire world exists, if pure consciousness does not exist, all else including mind will be non-existent. In other words, the mind has no existence apart

---

[37] Thibaut, 1994, op. cit., pp. 144-45.

[38] Swami Gambhirananda, 2000, *Brahmasūtrabhāṣya of Śrī Śaṅkarācārya*, II.iii.32, p. 493.

[39] Grimes, 1992, *The Naiṣkarmayasiddhi of Sureśvara*, p. 18.

from pure consciousness.

According to Vedānta, anything other than *Ātman* (Self) must be non-conscious.[40] *Ātman* being pure consciousness, it may be said that anything other than pure consciousness (in the sense of *cit*) is unconsciousness (*acit*).[41] Since the mind happens to be the object of consciousness, it is treated as *jaḍa* (insentient).[42] This shows that treating the mind as unconscious (*jaḍa*) in Vedānta is basically a definitional problem. The mind in its functional form is both consciousness and unconsciousness. The same thing may be elaborated. The *cit* is pure consciousness, whereas mind is both: conscious and unconscious. In that, the substance of mind and matter both is *cit*, showing thereby the Supreme Consciousness and Pure Experience itself. "Mental process is a veiling or (relative) unveiling of *cit* which is itself unchanged. Consciousness appears, however, to undergo change because of the modifications of mind of which it is the changeless substratum."[43]

It seems that when the mind reaches at its base, which is known as sublimal or subconscious mind. This state of mind, opens the gate of pure consciousness, the Absolute Reality. In this state, one is really *cit* moving in *cit* (pure consciousness) existing in *cit* and functioning in *cit*.[44]

This is the stage, where consciousness reverts back to its innate tendency of concentricity. In other words, this is the stage, where one may perceive the light of pure consciousness (i.e. realization of *Ātman*).

The reverse side of concentricity or the integrated state is the differentiated aspect, in which manifestation of pure consciousness

---

[40] Swami Jagadananda, 2000, *Upadeśasāhasrī of Śrī Śaṅkarācārya*, p. 65.

[41] Woodroffe, 2001, op. cit., p. 103.

[42] Ibid., p. 114.

[43] Ibid., p. 112.

[44] Woodroffe, 2001, op. cit., p. 422.

takes place through the medium of mind. It means that the integrated consciousness becomes differentiated consciousness due to the modifications of the mind, which creates not only duality of the knower and the known but also triplicity, the knower, the knowing and the known, with a view to gain experience of the world. But this is a relative state where pure consciousness being the Absolute Reality becomes the many due to modifications of the mind. In such a situation, pure consciousness (*cit*) is itself veiled. While manifesting through modifications of the mind, pure consciousness (*cit*) does not lose its capacity as the knower.[45] That is why according to Vedānta in the ultimate analysis, it is pure consciousness that is the knower, because without its reflection in the mind, the mind itself cannot gain experience of any kind.

DEFINING FOUR ASPECTS OF INTERNAL ORGAN, MANAS

"The *manas* is that modification of the internal instrument which considers the pros and cons of a subject (*saṁkalpa* and *vikalpa*)."[46] The mind with the organs of perception constitutes the mental sheath (*manomaya-kośa*).[47] It also coordinates the function of other senses.[48] By nature, "the mind is fickle and it is difficult to control."[49] It has twofold modifications: (i) the external modification assumes the form of "this", revealing thereby the external things, and (ii) the internal modification takes the form "I".[50] The former perceives the external objects through five organs as sound, touch, colour, taste and smell,[51] whereas the latter realizes the self in

---

[45] Woodroffe, 2001, op. cit., p. 115.

[46] Swami Nikhilananda, 1997, *Vedānta sāra*, verse 66, p. 46.

[47] Ibid., verse 74, p. 49.

[48] Ibid., verse 75, p. 49.

[49] Swami Swahananda, 2001, *Pañcadaśī of Śrī Vidyāraṇya Swami*, VII.120, pp. 283-84.

[50] Ibid., op. cit., X.7, p. 428.

[51] Ibid., X.8, p. 428.

the form "I". However, it has also been observed that "when the mind first contemplates external objects, it becomes *cittam* (i.e. consciousness)".[52]

Buddhi

It is treated as intellect, being that modification of internal instrument (*antaḥkaraṇa*), which determines the real nature of an object.[53] "This intellect (*Buddhi*) together with the organs of perception constitute the intelligent sheath (*vijñānamaya-kośa*).[54] This comparison does not seem to be appropriate for the obvious reason that, "the intellect itself is non-conscious, but it appears to be conscious like the black iron that appears to be red when charged with fire. It is illumined by the reflection of the Self without which it has no power of revealing things."[55] If that being the case, how the *Buddhi* being intellect can be compared with the *vijñānamaya-kośa*, which represents consciousness. It seems that the *vijñānamaya-kośa* is corresponding to consciousness (*cit*).

CITTA

As mentioned earlier, *citta* represents consciousness. It is also treated as the modification of the inner organ which remembers.[56] It is the storehouse of all the past impressions, tendencies, instincts, hereditary, traits, and *saṁskāras* (impressions).[57] In the commentary on the *Muṇḍaka Upaniṣad* (III.1.9), it is, however, stated that "reflecting mind (*citta*) thus has *cetana* behind it, energizing it to reflect and this *cetana* in its turn is interwoven by the fivefold *prāṇas*. The reflecting faculty left behind *citta* becomes as purified

---

52 Tilak, 2000, *Gita-Rahasya*, p. 183.

53 Swami Nikhilananda, 1997, op. cit., verse 65, p. 46.

54 Ibid., verse 72, p. 48.

55 Safaya, 1976, *Indian Psychology*, p. 217.

56 Swami Nikhilananda, 1997, op. cit., verse 68, p. 46.

57 Safaya, 1976, op. cit., p. 223.

cetana".[58] The *cetana* is consciousness.

EGO

According to Śaṅkara, "the ego-sense being grounded in the pure self does not prevent it from identifying itself (through Ignorance) with the body and organs with a sense of 'I' and 'mine'. Therefore, there is no change in the ego-sense even after the true nature of the object of the ego-sense has been established by reflective analysis."[59] This is known superimposition, interpreted as "I am this, this is mine". The ego is the first superimposition.[60] However, the ego-notion becomes the object for one who acts and experiences the individual soul.[61] Further, "when the ego-notion the seed of action present in the inner organ (mind) has been burnt up by the conviction, 'I am not ego', how can further action spring up".[62] This is replied as follows:

> Here, too, the ego-notion is said to be the seed of action. And action belongs to the one who has the ego-notion; the Self in the illusory form in which it appears capable of action. If the seed of action is burnt by the fire of knowledge, "I am not capable of action, the sprout of action will not appear" — this is the meaning of the verse.[63]

The ego-notion or the "I" appears when the modification of mind is directed to the external realm, according to Sureśvara in his *Naiṣkarmyasiddhi*. It is stated that:

> The Self or consciousness is present at all three levels or waking, dreaming and sleep. However, the "I" or ego-notion is present

[58] Swami Muni Narayana Prasad, 1998, *Muṇḍaka Upaniṣad*, p. 108.

[59] Swami Satchidanandendra, 1997, *The Method of Vedānta*, p. 413.

[60] Ibid., p. 412.

[61] Ibid., p. 422.

[62] Ibid.

[63] Ibid.

> only at the first two levels. It is not present in deep-sleep state. This proves that the "I" is not the Self. When the mind is present, then the "I" is present. When the mind is absent the "I" is absent. However, the self is by definition, omnipresent.[64]

In this context, it is further observed that:

> The self is eternal. If the "I" belonged to the Self, then the "I" would also be eternal. This would render the Scripture futile. Not only would the Scripture's description of liberation be rendered void, but it would make its statements ridiculous.[65]

From the above quotations, it appears that the system of Sureśvara is different from Śaṅkara's exposition of ego-notion. Śaṅkara has referred to superimposition as basis of arising the ego-sense, whereas Sureśvara has defined the ego-notion as modification of mind.

It is recently observed that "Advaita holds that the ego or I is directly revealed by consciousness (*kevala-sākṣibhāva*) without intervention of mind".[66] This observation is just reverse to Sureśvara's concept that the ego-notion is the modification of mind. If there is mind, there is ego as mentioned earlier. Now let us see how the ego-notion is revealed by consciousness. In this context, it is stated:

> When I say, "I am ignorant of something", "That is unknown to me", it is on the basis of the direct evidence of the witnessing consciousness. In short, every kind of claim that we make — that something is known, or that something is unknown — is on the basis of transcendental consciousness, which reveals objects directly or through the intentional performance of the mind. The evidence of transcendental consciousness is intrinsically valid. It is, therefore, considered to be the principle of all principles, the

---

[64] Grimes, 1992, op. cit., pp. 98-99.

[65] Ibid., p. 103.

[66] Balasubramanian, 2004, "Advaita Vedānta on the Problem of Enworlded Subjectivity", p. 90.

> source of all our claims – claim to knowledge as well as claim to ignorance.[67]

MIND AND CONSCIOUSNESS IN BUDDHISM

Citta is involved in the mental activities of human beings. It is the centre of man's emotional nature, understanding, perceptual and cognitive activities. *Citta* is also used as, "personal identity or surviving entity from existence to existence".[68] It is the possessor of not only ordinary knowledge, but also knowledge of super mundane.[69] The most important aspect of *citta* is that it is both the subjective–objective aspects of consciousness or thinking. It is stated that, "as a seat and organ of thought, *citta* thinks of its object by arranging itself in a thought process. *Citta* is both the cause of a variety of mental effects and the resultant thought. It is the storehouse of mental seeds or the arsenal of dispositional properties."[70]

However, *citta* is functionally classified into three ways:

i. the affective aspect concerned with feeling;
ii. the cognitive aspect dealing with knowing, reasoning and perceiving; and
iii. the conative aspect concerned with willing and desiring.

It is stated that "these three aspects do not, of course, function separately. As mental processes, all three aspects operate all at once by way of concurrent action and interaction".[71]

This classification of *citta* has, however, been described more sharply in the manual of *Abhidhamma* in three ways: as agent, as instrument and as activity. As an agent, *citta* cognizes an object.

---

[67] Balasubramanian, 2004, op. cit., p. 90.

[68] Thanh, 2008, *The Mind in Early Buddhism*, p. 197.

[69] Ibid., p. 196.

[70] Ibid., p. 197.

[71] Thanh, 2008, op. cit., p. 129.

As instrument, it accompanies the mental factors to cognize the object. As an activity, *citta* is itself nothing other than the process of cognizing the object. The main purpose for defining *citta* in three ways is to show that it is *citta* rather than a self that performs the act of cognition.[72] Here *citta* has been referred to as consciousness.

Citta as cognizer has not been accepted by Mādhyamika. It is stated that the agent may be real where there is a single action accompanied by a variety of factors. In such a case one factor out of many factors may be performing some special function of its own in the production process. But in the case of definite cognition and pure sensation (*citta*), there is no such action. On the contrary, every part has its own separate function. Therefore, it becomes difficult to impute the part of an agent to pure sensation.[73] Recently, it is observed that it is misleading:

> To think of cognition (*viññāna*) as an agent that acts upon its objects by "cognizing" them. In the causal syntax of dependent arising, however, cognitive awareness does not cognize anything, it is simply an awareness that arises when requisite conditions come together. Cognitive awareness is thus not an act of cognition, it simply is cognitive awareness itself.[74]

That apart, the fact remains that in the *Abhidharmakośabhāṣyam*, it is *citta* which accumulates (*cinoti*). It is termed *manas* because it knows (*manute*). It is also termed *vijñāna* because it distinguishes its object (*ālambanam vijñānāti*). This shows that *citta*, *manas* and *vijñāna* are used as synonyms in the *Abhidharma* context.[75] Yet, they have been differentiated as follows:

> *Citta* functions as the selective principle of good or evil, and is ethically wholesome, or unwholesome. Mind functions as

[72] Bhikkhu Bodhi, 1999, *A Comprehensive Manual of Abhidhamma*, p. 27.

[73] Stcherbatsky, 2003, *The Conception of Buddhist Nirvāṇa*, pp. 156-57.

[74] Waldron, 2003, *The Buddhist Unconscious*, p. 30.

[75] Pruden, 1991, *Abhidharmakośabhāṣyam*, chap. 2, p. 205.

> reflecting relation (thought) and as such remains as the object for the *citta* or consciousness. The *vijñānas* (the sensations) are recognized as inherent in the sense facilities. *Citta* deals with the entire world of consciousness expressed in various patterns of functions. It may be both pure (*anāsrava*) and impure (*sāsrava*). The entire extent of *citta* (consciousness) is indicated by the term *mana āyatana*. It is said that both *anāsrava prajñā* and *sāsrava manas* are included within *citta* (consciousness) in general. *Citta* (consciousness) remains from birth to death and continues till the achievement of *prajñā*. In a still wider significance *citta* is identified with internal principle. In that respect *citta* (consciousness) is recognized as the foremost internal factor. As such *citta* is associated, and linked with *vedanā* (feeling), *saṁjñā* (perception) and *saṁskāras* (impressions) *rūpa* (matter) and *citta* (consciousness) according to the *kośa* include the entire phenomenal and constituted world.[76]

The relationship between *citta* and *manas* (mind) is quite important in the sense that one cannot gain experience without mind. It is stated in the *Laṅkāvatārasūtra* that "the *manas* is not, however, an independent agent acting on *citta* from outside, it is indeed the creation of *citta* itself".[77] This fact is quite similar to Vedānta in which it is mentioned that the mind is created by consciousness.[78] However, the relationship between *citta* and *manas* is mentioned quite clearly in the *Laṅkāvatārasūtra* as follows:

> The *manas* walks along depending on the *citta*; the *citta* is caused to move by *vijñāna* and there is an interdependence among them. From this it is evident that the *manas* depends on the *citta* for its existence, and at the same time *citta* takes *manas* as the object of its activity. Without *manas* there will be no mentation, and without mentation *citta*'s own existence will not be known. The

---

[76] Haldar, 2001, *Some Psychological Aspects of Early Buddhist Philosophy Based on Abhidharmakośa of Vasubandhu*, pp. 60-61.

[77] Suzuki, 1999, *Studies in the Làṅkāvatāra Sūtra*, p. 250.

[78] Singh, 2004, op. cit., p. 74.

> one, thus, gives support to the other, and at the same time is supported by other.[79]

Citta has been described in the *Laṅkāvatārasūtra* in two ways: general and specific. In general way, it is the sum of all mental activities including both the mind proper and its various functions, whereas in a specific sense, "it is the principle of unification by which all activities are understood as issuing from one centre".[80] Further, "undifferentiated *citta* is divided into two parts: one is the seer and the other as the seen".[81] According to the *Laṅkāvatārasūtra*, the *citta* is rich in content, and just because of this inner richness, it is able to evolve out of itself a world of infinite multitudinousness. It is, indeed, an inexhaustible reservoir of seeds (*bīja*) which has been accumulated therein since beginningless past.[82] However, *citta* is treated as subconsciousness in the *Laṅkāvatārasūtra.*[83] *Citta* is also referred to as the absolute reality. This is evident from the statement that "suchness, emptiness, the limit, *nirvāṇa*, *dharmadhātu*, variety of will bodies — they are nothing but mind".[84] Here mind is referred to as *citta*. It is also stated that "*citta* is the Buddha".[85]

In another study, marked difference has, however, been observed between the mind and *citta*. It is stated that *mano* (mind) is not described having continuity, whereas consciousness is referred to as an unbroken stream. In this context, it is observed:

> Even *citta* came to be looked upon as a continuous process (*santati*, *santāna*) in the later Buddhist tradition but not *mano*. The reason of this is obvious. The Buddha did not deny the function of *mano*

[79] Suzuki, 1999, op. cit., p. 250.

[80] Ibid., p. 248.

[81] Ibid.

[82] Ibid., pp. 248-49.

[83] Ibid., p. 249.

[84] Ibid., p. 242.

[85] Ibid., p. 253.

in producing the feeling of self, i.e. the so-called empirical self. Yet he was not prepared to make this self either the pre-condition for all experience or a permanent and eternal entity.[86]

Concluding Remarks

The consciousness has been distinguished from the mind in the philosophy of Bart and Vedānta. Therefore, the mind–body problem may be easily resolved. This is mainly because both the mind and body exist in consciousness. It may, however be pointed out that the mind–body problem exists mainly in the philosophy of those philosophers, who do not make any distinction between the mind and consciousness.

[86] Kalupahana, 1992, *The Principles of Buddhist Psychology*, p. 31.

3

Consciousness in Advaita Vedānta

Introduction

Consciousness without self-consciousness is no consciousness at all. "Wherever it may be looked into, it has always a centre of self-awareness seeking to expand the circle of that centre as much as possible in one form or the other".[1] The self-consciousness has been explained in the metaphysical sense in the *Bṛhadāraṇyaka Upaniṣad* in the following observation:

> The *Bṛhadāraṇyaka Upaniṣad* traces the root of this feature of consciousness in the Supreme Being Himself. As it states in its own way, *Brahman* alone was there in the beginning. As such, though consciousness itself, it had nothing else beside itself to be conscious of. It, therefore, made itself the object of its consciousness and consequently became self-conscious. The world, according to the Upaniṣad, is nothing but that self-consciousness of *Brahman*. Since self-consciousness is instantaneous, the world got created instantaneously along with time and space themselves having come to serve only subsequently as factors of expansion and continuity involved in that act of creation from our viewpoint.[2]

In the case of human being, "self-consciousness is essentially a case of knowledge, it makes present to us our own Self. It is not a construction, it is not an illusion and therefore it is direct

---

[1] Singh, 2004, *Vedic Vision of Consciousness and Reality*, p. 266.

[2] Ibid., pp. 266-67.

knowledge."[3] Further, according to Udayana, "no prior experience is involved in one's being merely directly aware of oneself. Such self-awareness is always an immediate and original experience."[4] It may be stated that without self-consciousness (i.e. self-cognition) recollection of events is not possible. These observations suggest that self-consciousness (i.e. *jīvātman*) of human being becomes the centre of the universe. This self-consciousness is treated as foundational consciousness, on which perceptual knowledge is based according to Vedānta.

Self-consciousness and Knowledge

The most important aspect of the foundational consciousness is that it is treated as knowledge, according to Vedānta. It is explained below:

> There can be no objects of knowledge without knowledge. None can prove something that is not known, and the attempt to prove it would be as absurd as to maintain that there is no eye, though the form is apprehended. The objects may change their essence, but consciousness cannot be said to change inasmuch as it witnesses all objects irrespective of the place where they may happen to be; the fact of being known is thus implied by all objects without exception. Even when something is supposed to be non-existent, this very non-existence cannot be proved in the absence of knowledge.[5]
>
> The second feature of the Advaita analysis of consciousness lies in its insistence that consciousness is always distinct from the object of consciousness. The things, therefore, should on no account be identified with the consciousness which makes them its objects. From this follows two corollaries; namely — that consciousness cannot be its own object and that every object of consciousness is unconscious or material.[6]

[3] Stcherbatsky, 1996, *Buddhist Logic*, vol. II, p. 30.

[4] Chakrabarti, 2001, *Classical Indian Philosophy of Mind*, p. 271.

[5] Mukerji, 1938, *The Nature of Self*, p. 110.

[6] Ibid., pp. 110-11.

Consciousness has, however, been regarded as the ultimate principle of revelation for which alone the objects of the empirical world have become meaningful. In this context, it is observed that consciousness is "the centre of the whole world comprising the objects, the senses and the mind, and it has neither inside nor outside, it is altogether a mass of knowledge".[7]

This "occupies the central place of the universe, inasmuch as all objects owe their meaning and significance to the relations in which they stand to the self that essentially is consciousness".[8] It is known as "the Centre Theory of Self".

Consciousness as Foundational Knowledge

Pure consciousness is treated as the foundation on which existence gets unified with it. In that, the primacy of consciousness is admitted over the dynamics of existence.[9] It may be stated that "the notion of consciousness is so elementary that it cannot possibly be resolved into others more simple. It cannot, therefore, be brought under any genus — any more general conception; and consequently it cannot be defined. . . . It may, however, be philosophically analysed".[10] When the empirical contents are abstracted from the consciousness, one is likely to experience pure consciousness, being the Absolute Reality (i.e. *Brahman*). This is treated as the foundation through which the entire universe is known. Indeed it becomes difficult to comprehend such a simple entity to be treated as the Absolute Reality in Vedānta. In fact, the doubt has been raised that the existence of pure consciousness cannot be proved. In what follows is the brief discussion to justify pure consciousness as the Absolute Reality based on some scientific facts. It has been recently observed in science:

---

[7] Mukerji, 1938, op. cit., p. 112.

[8] Ibid.

[9] Singh, 2004, op. cit., p. 58.

[10] Bart, 1995, *Philosophy of Knowledge*, vol. I, pp. 191-92.

> The fourth of the great natural forces, in addition to gravity, electromagnetism and the strong nuclear force, is the weak nuclear force. . . . In spite of its unassuming name, the weak nuclear force, or weak force, is still more than a million billion billion billion times stronger than the force of gravity. Although such disparate strengths of the forces might be difficult to perceive, this variance is responsible for the universe's most desirable features, especially those that give rise to life. For example, if the force of gravity was not extremely weak compared to the other forces, the many atoms of which humans, planets, or stars consist would simply collapse upon each other.[11]

If one attempts to apply the above scientific observation to the sphere of consciousness, it is evident that the indeterminate, attributeless and differenceless pure consciousness may apparently be quite a weak force being subtle phenomenon as compared to the determinate consciousness possessing contents the empirical consciousness. But in reality, like the weak nuclear force, pure consciousness would be a much strong force than empirical consciousness. After all, empirical consciousness is nothing but the reflection of pure consciousness. The main function of consciousness is to reveal the objective side of the experience, although while revealing the object it reveals itself (*svaprakāśa*). However, pure consciousness reflects through the mind, which creates the subject and object duality in relation to the knowledge. In this process, the mind quite often obscures the light of consciousness through which it reveals the object. When empirical consciousness is abstracted from consciousness what remains is pure consciousness, which reveals quite sharply the object as well as itself. This seems to be the reason why the Advaita Vedānta treats pure consciousness as the Absolute Reality (i.e. *Brahman*). The determinate consciousness (i.e. empirical consciousness) is merely the reflection of pure consciousness.

Now modern physics shows that "when we penetrate the subatomic levels of reality down through the very fabric of space

---

[11] Bhaumik, 2005, *Code Name God*, pp. 140-41.

we will find that everything is interconnected".[12] Similarly when one purifies ones consciousness by withdrawing from the physical world, one is likely to experience pure consciousness through which not only everything is known but also one enters into time in the sense that previous births will be known. This has happened in the case of the Buddha who has seen his previous births through the purification of his consciousness. This suggests that by entering deeper into consciousness and reaching to the stage of pure consciousness, one enters into time and space. Therefore, an inference may be drawn that the treatment of pure consciousness as the Absolute Reality (*Brahman*) by the Upaniṣadic and the Vedāntic thinkers has some scientific basis, it is not merely a conjuncture or just a speculative idea.

Further, the distinction is made between pure consciousness (*Brahman*) in itself and pure consciousness (*Brahman*) in the universe. The *Brahman* itself is the transcendent beyond manifestation, whereas *Brahman* in the universe is the transcendent in manifestation.[13] The distinction between *Brahman* in universe and *Brahman* beyond manifestation may be illustrated in the following statement:

Brahman (Pure Consciousness) in Itself	*Brahman (Pure Consciousness in Universe) for Itself*
Ātman	*Jīvātman*
Indeterminate (*nirākāra* or (formless)) consciousness	Determinate (*sākāra*) form of consciousness
Integrated consciousness	Differentiated consciousness
Pre-reflective consciousness	Reflective consciousness
Witnessing consciousness	Witnessed consciousness
Mindless consciousness	Mindful consciousness
Sleeping state	Waking state

[12] Bhaumik, 2005, op. cit., p. 120.

[13] Radhakrishnan, 2009, *The Principal Upaniṣads*, p. 70.

The above distinctions are like two sides of one reality. In other words, pure consciousness being the one Absolute Reality becomes many in the manifestation which operates in the relative world. In fact, in the world, things are always changing in the process of becoming. What is constant in this process of becoming is pure consciousness being the Absolute Reality (*Brahman*). This has been summarized in the most elegant way: "what is incomplete in the relative world of becoming is complete in the absolute world of being".[14] Why pure consciousness is treated as the Absolute Reality because it becomes the theory of everything in perceiving the entire universe. It is also the unity of opposites.

The proof of pure consciousness is based on the deep-sleep experience. On waking from deep sleep, one recognizes that he has slept blissfully. On this evidence, the whole *brahma-vidyā* (i.e. the knowledge of the Absolute Reality) is based. Here the main purpose is briefly to show that the deep-sleep experience has been given due importance in knowing pure consciousness by Advaita Vedānta. Pure consciousness is, however, criticized as a fictitious entity. This is examined below.

Criticism of Pure Consciousness as a Fictitious Entity

Pure consciousness is treated as a fictitious entity on the following grounds:

i. Pure consciousness is a fictitious entity because it cannot manifest in any form.[15]

ii. Empirical awareness (awareness is nothing but consciousness) requires pure awareness (pure consciousness). In Advaita Vedānta, there is no logical connection between the two.[16]

iii. Our empirical consciousness can very well do the function

[14] Radhakrishnan, 2009, op. cit., p. 86.

[15] Rajagopal, 1993, *A Critique of Vedānta*, p. 71.

[16] Ibid., p. 46.

without pure consciousness.[17]

iv. Analysis of sleep experience is mistaken.[18]

We have already shown earlier the relationship between pure consciousness and empirical consciousness which is based not only on logic but it also has some scientific basis. This in a way shows that the criticisms referred to above have no substantial basis.

The author has contradicted his own statement. On the one hand, it is mentioned that our empirical consciousness can do without pure consciousness; on the other, it is said that reality is the process of change involving eternal forms. Now the question arises whether it is possible that the process of change can take place without consciousness? The answer is in the negative according to Vedānta. Even common sense shows that without consciousness no process of change can take place. It may, therefore, be inferred that the process of change is nothing but empirical consciousness. If the reality of the process of change requires some eternal forms, so will be the case with empirical consciousness. It also requires some eternal form, which is nothing but pure consciousness. If that is the case, how can pure consciousness be a fictitious entity? This shows that the author has not given sufficient thought to his critique of pure consciousness through which the entire universe is known. Indeed, pure consciousness happens to be the theory of everything as envisaged by the Upaniṣadic thinkers and the same is adopted by Advaita Vedānta.

However, for those who think that pure consciousness is a fictitious entity, certainly for them the analysis of sleep experience may be a mistaken entity as logical necessity. But the fact remains that pure consciousness persists in the deep-sleep state. It is known only when one awakes from sleep and says that I have slept well or I could not sleep well . This seems to be the reason for interpreting pure consciousness as witness consciousness in Advaita Vedānta. In

[17] Rajagopal, 1993, op. cit., p. 37.

[18] Ibid., p. 48.

what follows is a brief discussion regarding witness consciousness.

Consciousness as Witness

It has been observed that the witnessing consciousness does not perform any action and hence it is not an enjoyer or a sufferer. In that, it is mainly a disinterested onlooker.[19] This witnessing approach has been adopted mainly to show:

> Witnessing consciousness witnesses not merely what the individual does in his waking state but also the dream state and also the dreamless sleep. The consciousness that is aware of the "blank" of dreamless sleep, cannot ordinary experience of objects. Witnessing consciousness, which cannot go to sleep, is there to "know" the state of sleep.[20]

The idea of witnessing consciousness has been developed by the Yogācāra Buddhists. The concept of self-witness of consciousness (*svasaṁvitti-bhāga*) happens to be the essential substance of the consciousness and it itself gets transformed into *Ātman* (subjective aspect) and *dharma* (objective aspect).[21] It may be stated that the self-corroboratory aspect (*svasaṁvitti-bhāga*) is realized by the consciousness of itself. "If this was lacking, there would be no way of remembering, the manifestations of mind and its activities".[22] These observations are based on the concept of *ālaya-vijñāna* of the Yogācāra school of Buddhism.

The above observations resemble the deep-sleep experience of Advaita Vedānta. In the deep-sleep, pure consciousness persists, as a result when one wakes up from sleep one immediately remembers that, "I slept well and I do not know anything". This shows that remembering of the sleep experience becomes possible mainly because of the persistence of pure consciousness in deep sleep.

---

[19] Bhattacharyya, 2004, "Phenomenology and Indian Philosophy", p. 70.

[20] Ibid., p. 71.

[21] Ganguly, 1992, *Treatise in Thirty Verses on Mere Consciousness*, p. 77.

[22] Ibid., p. 139 fn. 15.

Pure consciousness has been used as witness consciousness in Advaita Vedānta. This happens to be the knower of three states of consciousness: deep-sleep, dream and waking. However, there is no difference between *Ātman* and *sākṣī* (witness) according to Śaṅkarācārya. It may be noted that later on a distinction between the two has been made.

Adhvarindra in his *Vedāntaparibhāṣā* has made a distinction between *Ātman* and *sākṣī*. The pure consciousness (eternal consciousness) is referred to as *Ātman*. When it is limited by the mind (*antaḥkaraṇa*), it becomes *jīva* (individual self). But when pure consciousness has the mind as its limiting adjunct (*upādhi*), it becomes *sākṣī* (witness consciousness). In the case of *jīva*, the mind is a qualifying attribute (*viśeṣana*). Whereas in the case of *sākṣī*, the mind is a limiting adjunct (*upādhi*).[23]

According to Vidyāraṇya Swami, the author of *Pañcadaśī*, pure consciousness is the inner principle, it is unchanged and unchangeable, therefore, immutable *kūṭastha*.[24] However, *kūṭastha* is also used as the witness consciousness.[25] The witness consciousness lights up the ego, the intellect and the sense objects. Even when ego, etc. are absent, it remains self-luminous as ever.[26] It may be noted that according to Vidyāraṇya, the witness consciousness (witness self) cannot be identified with the *jīva* which participates in life and affairs.[27]

Unity of Cit-Ātman (Pure Consciousness)

Brahman, *Ātman* and matter, explained through consciousness in such a logical and consistent framework, are rarely found in other

---

23 Adhvarindra, 2000, *Vedānta Paribhāsa*, pp. 37-38.

24 Swami Swahananda, 2001, *Pañcadaśī of Sri Vidyāraṇya Swami*, commentary on VIII.24, p. 358.

25 Ibid., VIII.25, p. 358.

26 Ibid., XII.12, p. 430.

27 Radhakrishnan, 1999, *Indian Philosophy*, vol. II, p. 602.

places. This is evident from the following observation:

> When the concentricity of consciousness remains in its innate status as holding to itself in the midst of the convulsions of the space–time continuum, it is called *Ātman*. The position in which it happens to break the barrier of space–time continuum by means of the power of its concentricity, it comes to be called *Brahman*. Lastly, when the concentricity of consciousness gets lost in the convulsion of the space–time continuum itself, it assumes the form of matter. Getting reduced to matter also, however, it tends to assert its concentricity in the formation of the particles out of the waves of energy followed by organization of the particles into atoms and eventually into living beings with their all out attempt to retain their individuality of conscious existence in all its concentricity. This is where *Ātman* reappears as *Jīvātman* with all possible distractions on the concentricity of consciousness in it on the one hand and the inverse attempt on its part to get revived it to the original one, on the other. This common tendency of the *jīva* to come to itself in the intensest possible concentricity of consciousness, goes veritably to suggest that concentricity is the innate tendency of consciousness.[28]

It is further explained that "*Ātman* is specific formulation of consciousness characterized by concentricity; when concentricity breaks down, *Ātman* becomes coincident either to *Brahman* upward or to matter below. But concentricity being innate to consciousness, its breakdown can never be absolute."[29]

Here it may be stated that the thought process (representing the self) has been compared to the atom by D.S. Kothari, the famous Indian physicist. This has been explained by the fact that in both, the thought process and the atom, there are no intermediate stages. One cannot deduct any stage, when an atom makes a transition from one stage to another. So is the case with the thought process. In fact, if one is aware of any intermediate stage in thought process,

---

[28] Singh, 2004, op. cit., pp. 255-56.

[29] Ibid., p. 255.

no thinking would be possible.[30]

The analogy of self with an atom is observed in another study. It is stated that "as the very being of the universe, pure existence is the man's innermost self. What is innermost in an atom must be innermost in man. By realizing one's true self one can realize that".[31] This may be explained through the Vedāntic concept of the material universe, which contains both: cosmic and individual. The former known as the macrocosmic is in essence the same as the latter described as the microcosmic. "The cosmos and the individual are made of the same stuff and show the same pattern."[32] Therefore, an inference may be drawn that the atom of material world may be experienced through the innermost self of human beings. In fact, this seems to be the reason why Sāṁkhya–Yoga philosophy states that the *guṇas* — *sattva, rajas* and *tamas* — are found in both: *prakṛti* (matter) and *puruṣa* (consciousness). This along with above analogy of the self with an atom indicates the most important viewpoint is that if consciousness is embodied in human beings, it may be found in the material universe too although it is very difficult to see and experience it. Based on the Vedāntic assertion that "whatever is in the body (*piṇḍa*) is also in the cosmos (*brahmāṇḍa*)",[33] an inference may be drawn that consciousness came from the material universe. Although it may surprise many, the fact remains that, "when the energy of the fundamental matter (*prakṛti*) gradually increases, it acquires the form of *caitanya* (consciousness) or the *Ātman.*"[34] This is reassured by a recent observation that consciousness grows out of matter only, when it became organic in process of evolution.[35]

---

[30] Kothari, 2002, "Atom and Self", p. 298.

[31] Swami Satprakashananda, 2004, *The Universe God and God-Realization from the Viewpoint of Vedānta*, p. 170.

[32] Swami Nikhilananda, 2008, *Self-Knowledge of Śrī Śaṅkarācārya*, p. 83.

[33] Tilak, 2000, *Gita-Rahasya*, pp. 200-01.

[34] Ibid., p. 218.

[35] Singh, 2004, op. cit., p. 17.

The above observation that consciousness grows of matter is, however, not acceptable even to Sāṁkhya philosophers.[36] Despite the fact that they have shown that the *guṇas* – *sattva, rajas* and *tamas* – are found in both *prakṛti* (matter) and *puruṣa* (consciousness). It seems that having accepted *prakṛti* and *puruṣa* as separate and independent entities, if they would accept the finding that consciousness grows out of matter, it would contradict their own position. But it is equally important to state that if they would have accepted the proposition the *prakṛti* and *puruṣa* came from the one substance as is the case with Vedānta, it would have not created any problem in establishing the interaction between *prakṛti* and *puruṣa*.

Now coming to another aspect of capturing the self through thought process in the analogy of self with atom as mentioned above, does not seem to be appropriate according to the Advaita Vedānta. This is mainly because "Śaṅkara argues that it is impossible for us to know the self by means of thought, since thought in itself is a part of the flux belonging to the region of non-self . . . yet we cannot think away from the self; for there is no consciousness or experience possible apart from it."[37] In fact, consciousness being the very essence of self, it shines itself and its awareness becomes immediate and direct. But when it manifests through the instrumentality of mind, the idea of ego enters in the mode of thought. In this process man lacks the true nature of his own self, but one gets immediate awareness of his own existence as "I am". In this context, it is stated that "I am" therefore "I think".[38] This is in quite contrast to Descartes's philosophy in which it is observed that "I think" therefore "I am" (*cogito ergo sum*). That apart, the fact remains that Descartes had tried to capture self through the thought process.

---

[36] Tilak, 2000, op. cit., p. 219.

[37] Radhakrishnan, 1999, op. cit., p. 476.

[38] Swami Satprakashananda, 2001, *Methods of Knowledge*, p. 83.

It may be stated that in Hegel's philosophy too thought and being are treated as identical.[39] The most important modern Indian thinker J. Krishnamurti has also equated thought with self. This is evident from the statement that "thought is the self, thought is the word which identifies itself as the 'me', and whatever level, high or low, the self is placed, it is still within the field of thought".[40] What is most surprising is that according to Krishnamurti "thought has created the thinker".[41] However, the position of Hegel and Krishnamurti happens to be just the reverse of the Vedāntic concept. According to Vedānta the thought process happens to be objective side of consciousness, whereas the self is being the subjective side of consciousness. Descartes and Hegel both have tried to capture the self through the thought process mainly because in Western philosophy self or consciousness is identified with mind. There is no difference between the two: consciousness (i.e. self) and mind. As a result, they have considered that thinking belongs to the self. Whereas in Indian thought self or consciousness is independent of mind. Self-consciousness (i.e. *jīvātman)* manifests through the mind which thinks. Therefore, the thinking (or thought) does not seem to be appropriate measure to capture the self according to Vedānta philosophy.

The Hegelian concept of identification of thought with being is also not acceptable to the Buddhists. In this context it is stated that, "in Buddhism, however, thought and being are not identical. Being, which is *vithi mutta*, is opposed to thought, *vithi citta*. Though there is thus a contrariety, yet there is a similarity between the two, in that both are subjective."[42] However, according to Vedānta there is no difference between self and consciousness. The distinction between the two has been allowed mainly because when the emphasis is given to the self in relation to objects, the term consciousness has

---

[39] Hegel, 1998, *Phenomenology of Spirit*, p. 33.

[40] Krishnamurti, 1992, *Choiceless Awareness*, p. 97.

[41] Ibid., p. 39.

[42] Aung, 1979, *Compendium of Philosophy*, p. 9.

been used. When we speak of the "Self" simply, we do not want to emphasize that relation.[43] The fact remains that the self and consciousness are one. The self is eternal consciousness by its very nature.[44]

The unity of consciousness in the above observation is based on the philosophical jargon. As a result, it becomes too complicated to be understood by a common man. However, Śaṅkarācārya has explained very precisely how the same consciousness works in different activities of the human being. It is observed:

> Existence-knowledge through which all things in dream are known is the knower. It is the same entity that is known in dream by Māyā. It is the same consciousness through which one sees, hears, speaks, smells, tastes, touches and thinks in that state is respectively called the eye, the ear, the larynx, the auditive organ, the tongue, the organ of touch and the mind. Similarly, it is the same consciousness that becomes in dream the other organs also functioning variously.[45]

Nature of Reality

According to Vedānta, the reality is uncaused, it does not undergo any change. Further, it is neither dependent on nor be contradicted by anything. The reality is self-existent and it is beyond time, space and causality. In fact, "Reality is eternal, infinite, absolute existence. Vedānta identifies reality with being. Whatever fails to be has but apparent existence and is therefore unreal. . . . What is fleeting is unreal, what is constant is real."[46] However, the ultimate reality is existence (*sat*), consciousness (*cit*) and bliss (*ānanda*).

---

[43] Thibaut, 1994, op. cit., pp. 120-21.

[44] Swami Gambhirananda, 2000, *Brahmasūtrabhāṣya of Śrī Śaṅkarācārya* II.3.18, pp. 476-77.

[45] Swami Jagadananda, 2000, *Upadeśasāhasrī of Śrī Śaṅkarācārya* XVII.14-15, p. 195.

[46] Swami Satprakashananda, 2001, op. cit., p. 165.

The reality is existence (*sat*). This could be supported by the *Bhagavadgītā* in which it is stated, "of the unreal, there is no existence, of the real there is no non-existence. The final truth of both of these is known by the man of wisdom."[47] Therefore, an inference may be drawn that the real never goes out of existence, whereas "the unreal is a mere form or appearance without being, it appears and disappears".[48] However, "existence implies consistency and the world lacks consistency, it is unreal".[49] The real is devoid of parts and has no modification.[50] The difference between objects of the same class have no reference to the concept of *sat*. Whereas *Brahman* is the absolute reality, without name and form.[51] From II.24 of *Pañcadaśī*, an inference has been drawn that "*sat* does exist, for nobody doubts its own existence. If *sat* is many it cannot be unlimited. Moreoever, the one *sat* appears *vyavahārika* and *prātibhāsika*."[52]

Consciousness (*cit*) meets the most important criterion of reality, namely, non-contradiction. The real does not contradict itself nor is it contradicted by anything else.[53] In this context, it has been pointed out that there is only consciousness which cannot be contradicted with absolute certainty. This is mainly because of the fact that even the absence of consciousness has to be testified by consciousness itself. It is stated that, "consciousness alone does not appear to be; it is. For, in the case of consciousness, appearance and reality coincide".[54] Here, it may be mentioned that pure

---

[47] Sri Sri Paramahansa Yogananda, 2007, *The Bhagavad Gītā*, vol. I, II.16, p. 206.

[48] Swami Satprakashananda, 2004, op. cit., p. 165.

[49] Safaya, 1976, *Indian Psychology*, p. 204.

[50] Swami Swahananda, 2001, op. cit., II.22, p. 39.

[51] Ibid., II.23, p. 40.

[52] Ibid.

[53] Swami Satprakashananda, 2004, op. cit., p. 167.

[54] Mohanty, 1995, "Some Aspects of Indian Thinking on Being", p. 150.

consciousness itself is reality,[55] its appearance or manifestation is changing and negatable. Further, pure consciousness is reality, which is ever unborn, immovable and free from the character of materiality: it is all peace and non-dual.[56] In fact, pure consciousness happens to be both: *Brahman* and *Ātman* as mentioned earlier. It has been observed that according to Śaṅkara, "Consciousness as eternal, transcendent existence is unchanging, uncaused and homogeneous".[57]

Reality also happens to be bliss (*ānanda*). Pure consciousness is the *Ātman*.[58] This is the eternal witness of all changes. It is devoid of parts, unattached, pure and subject to no modification. It is bliss eternal.[59] It is stated that "as the *Ātman* is the object of supreme love, it follows that happiness which is inherent in the *Ātman*. Bliss is not only natural to the *Ātman*; it is also its distinctive feature."[60] However, supreme bliss is indivisible and homogeneous and in that it is *Brahman* itself.[61] This suggests that bliss is pure consciousness, because it is un-divisible and homogeneous.

We have described *sat-cit-ānanda* separately in the above description of reality. However, the fact remains that *sat-cit-ānanda* happen to be one essential content of the self (*Ātman)*, the immortal reality.

> As *Sat* it exists; as *Cit*, it is conscious of itself and of everything that emanates from it (nothing in this world exists other than what emanates from the one reality); as *Ānanda*, it creates and

[55] Swami Nikhilananda, 2000, *The Māṇḍūkya Upaniṣad with Gauḍapāda's Kārikā and Śaṅkara's Commentary*, V.7, p. 55.

[56] Ibid., Gauḍapāda's *Kārikā* 45, p. 262.

[57] Indich, 2000, *Consciousness in Advaita Vedānta*, p. 26.

[58] Swami Tattwananda, 2002, *The Quintessence of Vedānta of Śrī Śaṅkarācārya*, V.457, p. 166.

[59] Ibid, V.458, p. 166.

[60] Ibid., V.623, p. 234.

[61] Swami Swahananda, 2001, op. cit., V.XV.2, p. 552.

> feels all pleasures and pains. As *Sat-Cit* it exists and is aware of the infinite potential latent in itself and in its insurmountable urge to actualize it. It unfolds itself assuming the form of all objects and subjects, all perceptual experiences, and the pleasures and pains that go with them.[62]

It may, however, be pointed out that all the three — *sat-cit-ānanda* are manifesting in *sāttvika vṛttis*.[63] whereas *sat-cit* reflect in *rājasika* and *tāmasika vṛtti*s of intellect. In the inert objects like clay and stone, only existence is manifesting.[64]

Sat, cit, ānanda are also known as *pratyagātman* (pure consciousness). "It is at once *sat* or the true, and *nitya* or the eternal; for its existence is not negated during any one of three levels of consciousness."[65] These three levels are dreamless sleep, dream and waking. However, a similar concept known as *pratyātmāryajñāna* has been used in Zen Buddhism based on the *Laṅkāvatārasūtra*. This has been defined as supreme wisdom realized in the inmost depths of consciousness, which is something defying all description and altogether unpredictable. Therefore, it could be dealt with by Dharmata Buddha himself.[66]

It is thus evident that *sat-cit-ānanda*, being the ultimate reality, is known as *Brahman* or *Ātman*. However, according to Vedānta, existence and consciousness happen to be one because it is contended that "existence itself is the same as consciousness, and

---

[62] This statement is based on the commentary on V.II.i.3 of the *Kaṭha Upaniṣad*. See Swami Muni Narayana Prasad, 2004, *Kaṭha Upaniṣad*, p. 83.

[63] The word *vṛtti* is derived from the root *vṛt* meaning thereby "to exist". In that, *vṛtti* is a way of existing in which generally modifications, states, activities or its functions are considered. However, in the present context it would more appropriate to translate *vṛtti* as modifications or functionings; see Taimni, 1999, *The Science of Yoga*, p. 8.

[64] Swami Swahananda, 2001, op. cit., V.XV-21 and XV-20, p. 558.

[65] Swami Tattwananda, 2002, op. cit., V.610, p. 228.

[66] Suzuki, 1999, *Studies in the Laṅkāvatāra Sūtra*, p. 146.

also that the consciousness itself is existence".[67] No attempt has been made to explain why both are one. The main reason for treating the existence and consciousness as one is that consciousness happens to be the biggest unity. As a result, it is treated as a unified theory of everything. It is stated that, "the foundation lies in the unification of consciousness with existence in the basic nature of the Reality and admittance of the primacy of consciousness over the dynamics of existence. Without admitting consciousness as the coordinate of existence, neither existence will have any validity nor dynamics will have any reason behind its propulsion."[68] It has been further explained that, "consciousness brings awareness of existence, can penetrate into it any extent and must, therefore, be the subtlest form, if not of existence as such, at least of existents in all possible forms. On account of this quality of it, it seems to be the closest associate of existence."[69] However, in view of this observation, it may now be possible to reconcile the criticisms regarding the existence and consciousness, which are discussed below.

Existence and Consciousness

It is stated:

> The existence is found to be absolute ground of the phenomenal existence of all things and the consciousness is found to be the absolute ground of the manifestation of all the things - the existence is the sole supporter and the Consciousness is the sole revealer of the entire universe of thought and existence. Now, the question arises, what is the relation between the Existence and the Consciousness? The exponents of the view in question assert they are not two Realities, but one and identical.[70]

---

[67] Swami Gambhirananda, 2000, op. cit., III.ii.21, p. 618.

[68] Singh, 2004, op. cit., p. 58.

[69] Ibid., p. 60.

[70] Sadhu Santinatha, 1938, *The Critical Examination of the Philosophy and Religion*, vol. II, p. 530.

CRITICISM

The above concept is criticized on the following grounds:

i. The identity between two entities: Existence and consciousness cannot be established because "Existence refers to being, and consciousness refers to knowing: Existence is that which is, and Consciousness is that which knows: Existence is Substance, and Consciousness is Subject. Being and knowing cannot be regarded as the same phenomenon."[71]

ii. If Existence and Consciousness may be regarded one as the attribute of the other, "it is relation of identity (*tādāmya*) that is established, but not their absolute oneness, and hence the differenceless, attributeless non-duality of the ground of the existence and revelation of the world of diversities is not proved".[72]

RECONCILIATION

According to Advaita Vedānta, being is consciousness and knowing is also consciousness. Therefore, being and knowing are not different but both are one. This has been accepted by the author as relation of identity. But how can the differenceless and attributeless non-duality become the absolute oneness as the ground of existence and revelation of the world diversities is discussed below:

The differenceless and attributeless is nothing but pure consciousness, which is treated as the *Brahman* being the Absolute Reality. This has been justified on the ground that

> Existence apart from Universal Consciousness has no meaning, for existence is always associated with awareness of a being or entity by itself or by others. Hence pure Existence and pure consciousness are synonymous. . . . The existence of the universe apart from universal consciousness cannot be proved or asserted, for he who has to prove it, and him to whom it is to be proved, are

[71] Sadhu Santinatha, 1938, op. cit., p. 533.

[72] Ibid., p. 535.

themselves objects of consciousness and part of the universe.[73]

It may, further, be stated that in consciousness both, individual and universal can exist without objects as has been the case with the experience of deep sleep. However, such experience may also be realized in *samādhi* (transcendental state). Therefore, "consciousness is primary in experience, and consciousness of objects secondary. Hence the universe has no permanent or independent existence of its own apart from Universal consciousness, and as such is only appearance in Universal consciousness."[74]

In the Upaniṣads, the Absolute Reality, i.e. *Brahman* referred to as non-dual and the origin of everything happens to be the pure Subject and therefore is beyond the reach of words and thought.[75] It is defined as *neti-neti* (not this not this). In this sense it becomes attributeless (*nirguṇa*). However, the Vedānta has recognized two orders of Reality: the transcendental and the empirical, the former is the Absolute and the latter is the relative. It may be noted that from the empirical plane being the experience of duality, the absolute reality of non-dual may be difficult to know. Yet, it is not beyond experience, as is evident from the following observation:

> Being the Reality and the source of all phenomena, it is not an entity beyond experience. It is the inner self (*Pratyak-Ātman*) of all, the eternal Subject. It is self-cognized within phenomena; that is, it is intuitively cognized, directly and immediately, as the pure Witness Self (*sākṣī*) within by all beings. It is the Ground and Source of all objective experience, internal or external, on the phenomenal plane, just as one is aware of one's eyes without seeing them, for they enable one to see all things. This is the noumenal point of view. All phenomena are revealed by, and get their validity from the Self, which is pure Witness Subject in all.[76]

[73] Swami Mukhyananda, 2006, *Sri Shankaracharya*, pp. 100-101.

[74] Ibid., p. 102.

[75] Ibid., p. 49.

[76] Ibid., pp. 49-50.

The pure witness subject is nothing but pure consciousness which one may get by abstracting from empirical consciousness all the limitations like mind and matter. In that, it becomes mindless and bodiless (i.e. removing involvement of consciousness in material things) consciousness.[77] This pure consciousness is treated as the Absolute Reality, which in turn is referred to as the *Brahman* or the *Ātman* in Advaita Vedānta. It may be explained by taking the instance of an individual human being who never exists a moment without thinking about his plan of work in the mind to actualize it. In fact, every human being searches constantly "for the new avenues of self-expression, so that one can actualize for oneself the self content of Happiness. By extension of the farthest limit, what is true for the individual is also true for the Absolute Reality."[78]

The existence of consciousness lies in the never-ending functional states of its manifestation. In every functional state, it attains a new form. It takes numerous forms. In fact, it is stated:

> There is no actual state in which consciousness is functionless. Unmanifest consciousness, as reality behind all the functional states, is only a verticalized version, or an abstraction. When the same is seen horizontally it appears as the manifest world. What is called creation here is only the process by which the vertical or abstract Reality becomes horizontalized and attains a manifest form. It is nothing other than the unfoldment of the endless creative urge inherent in the Self or Consciousness.[79]

Causal Body of Human Being and Causal Consciousness

CAUSAL BODY

It is observed that "the causal body owes its name to the fact that in it reside the causes which manifest themselves as effects in the

---

[77] Woodroffe, 2001, *The World as Power*, p. 303.

[78] Swami Muni Narayana Prasad, 2009a, *The Taittirīya Upaniṣad*, p. 137.

[79] Ibid., p. 138.

lower planes".[80] This is mainly because the experiences of past lives are stored in the causal body, which has two main functions:

i. "To act as a vehicle for the Ego: the causal body is the body of *Manas*, the form aspect of the individual, the true man, the Thinker."[81]

ii. "To act as a receptacle or storehouse for the essence of the man's experiences in his various incarnations. The causal body is that into which is woven everything which can endure, and in which are stored the germs of qualities, to be carried over the next incarnation."[82]

Every individual has a causal body, which constitutes individuality. This body will last through the whole of the human evolution. It is observed that, "the causal body is a true register — *the only true register* — of the growth of the man of the stage of evolution to which he has attained".[83] However, the causal body is the organ for abstract thinking. "In the thinker, thus, is the store of experiences, reaped in all our past lives, harvested through many rebirths."[84]

The following observations regarding the causal body may be worth stating:

i. The causal body is the form aspect of the individual. In this context, it may be noted that when by the power of the Self preparing its own habitation, the matter of the mind plane begins slowly to evolve, then there is a downpouring from the great ocean of *ātman-buddhi*, which is ever brooding over the evolution of man, and this, as it were, meets the upward-growing, unfolding mind stuff, comes into union with it,

---

[80] Powell, 2000, *The Causal Body and the Ego*, p. 89.

[81] Ibid.

[82] Ibid.

[83] Ibid., p. 90.

[84] Ibid., p. 91.

and at that point of union the causal body, the individual, is formed.[85]

ii. Life after life, century after century, millennium after millennium, this evolution of individual proceeds, and in aiding its growth by conscious effort we are working in harmony with the divine will, and carrying out the purpose for which we are here. Nothing good that is once woven into the texture of this causal body is ever lost; nothing is dissipated; for this is the man who lives forever.[86]

The causal body is treated as repository of kārmic impressions which are accumulated in the course of many lives. In this context, the following observations are worth noting:

> Out of this dense store there arise not only the characteristics that determine each individual being but also the forms that appear in his or her consciousness in the shape of the empirical world-forms, moreover, that are shared with other members of our species and even to some extent with other species whose world-experience is in part similar to our own. Thus behind the conscious mind there lies a vast hinterland of unconscious memory, which is the real source of each individual being. Rebirth comes about when a group of accumulated impressions or "Kārmic seeds" (*karmabījas*) come together and stir into activity, while a further group (forming *sañcita-karma*) remains dormant. The awakening impressions form *prārabdha-karma*, the portion of *karma* that finds expression in course of a single lifetime; emerging from the causal body in the shape of formative forces (*saṁskāras*) — predisposed capacities and patterns of thought and behaviour — they constitute the subtle body of the new individual being. *Prārabdha-karma*, once launched into manifestation, must play itself out: even the liberated (*jīvanmukta*), until physical death, remains subject to *prārabdha-karma*, which, like an arrow

[85] Besant, 2000, *Man and His Bodies*, p. 107.

[86] Ibid., p. 114.

once has left the bow, must complete its course.[87]

CAUSAL CONSCIOUSNESS

It is explained as:

> Causal consciousness thus deals with the essence of a thing, whilst the lower mind studies its details. With the mind, we talk round a subject, or endeavor to explain it; with the causal consciousness, we take up the essence of the idea of the subject, and move it as a whole, as one moves a piece when playing chess. The causal plane is a world of realities: we no longer deal with emotions, ideas or conceptions, but with thing in itself.[88]

The thinker, with his causal consciousness dwells within himself, engrossed with deeper aspects of life and thought, "seeking to understand causes rather than troubling himself with effects, and approaching nearer and nearer to the recognition of the One that underlies all the diversities of external nature".[89] It is, further, explained as follows:

> It is only when consciousness has withdrawn from the lower bodies, and is once more centered in the ego, that the final result of the incarnation just concluded is known. Then it is seen what new qualities he has acquired in that particular little cycle of his evolution. At that time also, a glimpse of the life as a whole is obtained: the ego has for a moment a flash of clearer consciousness, in which he sees the result of the life just completed, and something of what will follow from it in his next birth.[90]

Concluding Remarks

Pure consciousness being the one Absolute Reality becomes many

---

[87] Cross, 2014, *Schopenhauer's Encounter with Indian Thought*, p. 140.

[88] Powell, 2002, op. cit., p. 105.

[89] Ibid., p. 106.

[90] Ibid., p. 129.

in the manifestation, which operates in the phenomenal world (*saṁsāra*). According to Vedānta, it is the self-consciousness through which all the things are known, is the knower. It is the same entity that is known in dream, referred to as creativity of consciousness. In dreamless sleep, the same self-consciousness becomes witnessing consciousness (*sākṣī*). Further, the self-consciousness works through eyes, ears, the organ of touch and the mind.

When self-consciousness manifests through the mind, it becomes the phenomenal consciousness. Therefore, in Vedānta the phenomenal consciousness is explained through self-consciousness. It may be noted that the phenomenal consciousness is not different from self-consciousness, because the former is nothing but manifestation of the latter. Further, there is no mind–body problem in Vedānta. This is mainly because both mind and body happen to be the objects of self-consciousness.

The most important aspect of Vedānta philosophy is that all the manifestation of universe is a play of pure consciousness being the Absolute Reality, which is known as *Brahman*.

The concept of causal body of Vedānta is, however, quite important because it lasts through the whole of the human evolution. It persists through successive rebirths determined by the law of *karma* (action).

4

Consciousness in Jean-Paul Sartre's Philosophy of Existentialism

Introduction

IN SARTRE's philosophy, man has been placed at the supreme position, mainly because he creates his own world to live in. In man, existence precedes essence. Man is defined by Sartre as the for-itself, which is consciousness and it is contrasted with "the in itself", i.e. matter. However, Sartre's exploration of man's nature and his possibilities is quite unique in the sense that consciousness is treated as nothingness. Yet, consciousness has become the Absolute Reality. Further, "by nature all consciousness is self-consciousness".[1] The other important fact is that consciousness is characterized by spontaneity, absoluteness and transparency.[2]

Characteristics of Consciousness

SPONTANEITY

According to Sartre, "transcendental consciousness is an impersonal spontaneity. It determines itself to exist at every instant, without us being able to conceive of everything before it. Thus, every instant of our conscious lives reveals to us a creation *exnihilo.*"[3] It is further observed that "spontaneity renders impossible any

---

[1] Sartre, 1984, *Being and Nothingness*, p. xi.

[2] Medhidhammaporn, 1995, *Sartre's Existentialism and Early Buddhism*, p. 42.

[3] Sartre, 2012, *The Transcendence of the Ego*, p. 46.

distinction between action and passion, and any conception of any conception of an autonomy of the will".[4] On this level, "man considers himself to be simultaneously both subject and object.[5] However, being spontaneous or self-caused consciousness is said to be free, because it is not subject to any causal laws.[6] "Consciousness takes fright at its own spontaneity because it senses that it lies beyond freedom."[7] It is stated:

> The spontaneity of consciousness cannot emanate from the "I", it goes towards the "I", it meets it, it allows it to be glimpsed under its limpid thickness but it is given above all as an *individuated* and *impersonal* spontaneity.[8]

ABSOLUTENESS

It is stated that "the existence of consciousness, indeed, is an absolute, because consciousness is conscious of itself; in other words, the type of existence that consciousness has is that it is consciousness of itself".[9] According to Sartre, consciousness is a revealing intuition of something.[10] "It is not revealed by anything other than itself. Consciousness is self-luminous or self-transparent."[11] However, consciousness being absolute, is non-substantial, mainly because its "existence precedes essence".[12] This is explained:

> Consciousness has nothing substantial, it is pure "appearance" in the sense that it exists only to the degree to which it appears.

---

[4] Sartre, 2012, op. cit., p. 48.

[5] Ibid.

[6] Medhidhammaporn, 1995, op. cit., pp. 42-43.

[7] Sartre, 2012, op. cit., p. 47.

[8] Ibid., p. 46.

[9] Ibid., p. 7.

[10] Sartre, 1984, op. cit., p. 786.

[11] Medhidhammaporn, 1995, op. cit., p. 43.

[12] Ibid.

> But it is precisely because consciousness is pure appearance, because it is total emptiness (since the entire world is outside it) — it is because of this identity of appearance and existence within it that it can be considered as the absolute.[13]

SELF-CONSCIOUSNESS

The pre-reflective cogito is non-positional self-consciousness.[14] It is stated that "the very nature of consciousness is such . . . that for it to be and to know itself are one and the same . . . Consciousness of an object is consciousness of being conscious of an object. Thus by nature all consciousness is self-consciousness."[15] However, self-consciousness is regarded as the only "mode of existence".[16] This indicates that "the type of existence that consciousness has is that is consciousness of itself".[17] From these observations, it follows that "self-consciousness is the necessary condition of the existence of consciousness".[18] Thus self-consciousness is taken to be an essential characteristic, which differentiates consciousness from a non-conscious being.[19]

However, the reduction consciousness involves the subject-object dualism, which is typical of knowledge. If one accepts the knower–known dyad, it may lead to an infinite regress. In order to avoid this infinite regress, Sartre has suggested that "consciousness of self is not dual. If we wish to avoid an infinite regress, there must be an immediate, non-cognitive relation of the self to itself."[20] This consciousness is known as self-consciousness under which the

---

[13] Sartre, 1984, op. cit., p. 17.

[14] Ibid., pp. xi-xii.

[15] Ibid., p. xi.

[16] Ibid., p. 14.

[17] Sartre, 2012, op. cit., p. 7.

[18] Medhidhammaporn, 1995, op. cit., pp. 43-44.

[19] Ibid., p. 44.

[20] Sartre, 1984, op. cit., p. 12.

subject–object duality does not arise.[21]

According to Sartre, self-consciousness is not a new consciousness, "but as the only mode of existence which is possible for consciousness of something".[22] This shows that self-consciousness and consciousness are mutually dependent.[23] It is, further, observed that "consciousness exists as a circle: consciousness transcends itself and knows the object, but this can do only if it is self-consciousness".[24] The other fact is that "an intention, a pleasure, a grief can exist only as immediate self-consciousness".[25]

Another important observation is that, "I am at once consciousness of the being and self-consciousness".[26] This self-consciousness may be fairly comparable to Vedānta, which treats self-consciousness as *jīvātman* (self).[27]

TRANSPHENOMENAL BEING

According to Sartre, consciousness has two defining characteristics: intentionality and self-transparency. Consciousness is consciousness of something[28] and consciousness of something is self-consciousness.[29] "Self-consciousness presupposes consciousness of something for the reason that consciousness is aware only when it is consciousness of something. And consciousness of something, in turn, presupposes the being of object."[30] Consciousness of something, according to Sartre, is explained below:

---

[21] Medhidhammaporn, 1995, op. cit., p. 44.

[22] Sartre, 1984, op. cit., p. 14.

[23] Medhidhammaporn, 1995, op. cit., p. 44.

[24] Roy, 2013, *Subjectivity of Science*, p. 121.

[25] Sartre, 1984, op. cit., p. 14.

[26] Ibid., p. 794.

[27] Swami Satprakashananda, 2001, *Methods of Knowledge*, p. 91.

[28] Sartre, 1984, op. cit., p. xxxi.

[29] Ibid., p. 579.

[30] Medhidhammaporn, 1995, op. cit., p. 46.

> A revealing intuition of something — i.e. of a transcendent being. Now only does pure subjectivity, if initially given, fail to transcend itself to posit the objective: a "pure" subjectivity disappears. What can properly be called subjectivity is consciousness (of) consciousness. But this consciousness (of being) consciousness must be qualified in some way, and it can be qualified only as revealing intuition or it is nothing. Now a revealing intuition implies something revealed. Absolute subjectivity can be established only in the face something revealed: immanence can be defined only within the apprehension of a transcendent.[31]

However, "consciousness implies in its being a non-conscious and transphenomenal being. In particular there is no point in replying that in fact subjectivity implies objectivity and that it constitutes itself in constituting the objective: we have seen that subjectivity is powerless to constitute the objective".[32] This shows that we have left pure appearance and have arrived at full being. Consciousness is a being whose existence posits its essence, and inversely it is consciousness of a being, whose essence implies its existence; that is, in which appearance lays claim to being.

"Being is everywhere."[33] In this respect, it is stated that, "being is no other than the transphenomenal being of phenomena and not a noumenal being which is hidden behind them".[34]

Classification of Being

Two separate regions of being have been distinguished by Sartre. These are: Being for-itself (consciousness) and Being in-itself (matter). These regions are referred to as the distinction between consciousness and its object. Sartre has insisted that these two different types of being "that there are two types of existence, as

---

[31] Sartre, 1984, op. cit., p. 23.

[32] Ibid., pp. 23-24.

[33] Ibid., p. 24.

[34] Ibid.

thing-in-the world and as consciousness, is an ontological law".[35]

BEING IN-ITSELF

It is stated that "the in-itself has nothing secret: it is solid (massif). In a sense we can designate it as synthesis. But it is the most indissoluble of all: the synthesis of itself with itself."[36] Being is itself. "It is an immanence which cannot realize itself, an affirmation which cannot affirm itself an activity which cannot act, because it is glued to itself."[37] This is explained below:

> If being is in itself, this means that it does not refer to itself as self-consciousness does. It is this self. It is itself so completely that the perpetual reflection which constitutes the self is dissolved in an identity.[38]

The in-itself does not admit any change or becoming. This is evident from the fact that, "transition, becoming, anything which permits us to say that being is not yet what it will be and that it is already what it is not-all that is forbidden on principle".[39] The in-itself is also "uncreated without reason for being, without any connection with another being: being in-itself is *de trop* for eternity".[40]

BEING FOR-ITSELF

The for-itself is such that, "there is being. The character of a phenomenon comes to being through the for itself. . . . It has the right to turn back on itself toward its own origin."[41] It is, however, stated that "if the for itself is a Nothingness, then in what sense is

---

[35] Medhidhammaporn, 1995, op. cit., p. 47. It may be noted that this observation is based on Jean-Paul Sartre's book *Imagination: A Psychological Critique*, 1962, p. 116.

[36] Sartre, 1984, op. cit., p. 28.

[37] Ibid., p. 27.

[38] Ibid., p. 28.

[39] Ibid., p. 29.

[40] Ibid.

[41] Ibid., p. 788.

it Being".[42] It is explained in the following observation:

> If, they say, a single one of the atoms which constitute the universe annihilated, there would result a catastrophe which would extend to the entire universe and this would be, in particular, the end of the Earth and the solar systems. This metaphor can be of use to us here. The for itself is like a tiny nihilation which has its origin at the heart of Being: and this nihilation is sufficient to cause a total upheaval to happen to the in-itself. This upheaval is the world.[43]

THE FOR-ITSELF AND THE IN-ITSELF: THEIR RELATIONSHIPS

The relation between the for-itself and the in-itself constitutes the world. To establish a bond between them appears at first glance difficult to establish. But Sartre has stated that the relation between them is a primitive upsurge, "and it forms a part of the very structure of these beings. The concrete is revealed to us as the synthetic totality of which consciousness, like the phenomenon, constitutes only the articulations."[44] Here the key to the relation is the for-itself rather than the in-itself, because the for-itself is referred to as knowing. Thus, consciousness of a being is such that "in its being, its being is in question in so far as this being implies a being other than itself."[45]

Now the problem is that why the being for-itself has to be a knowledge of the in-itself? This is mainly because both: the for-itself and the in-itself cannot be considered in isolation. The for-itself (consciousness) in isolation is abstraction, as the consciousness is consciousness of something. The in-itself (matter) also does not have any meaning unless it is appearing to consciousness. In this context, it may be stated that the knowledge of the matter

[42] Sartre, 1984, op. cit., p. xxv.

[43] Ibid., p. 786.

[44] Ibid., p. 238.

[45] Ibid., p. 239.

(the in-itself) is mainly through perception, which is related to consciousness.

The relationship between the in-itself and the for-itself through the trinity into Hegelian terms as mentioned by Sartre, is presented in the following statement.

Trinity	*Concepts*
Thesis	The in-itself (matter)
Antithesis	The for-itself (consciousness)
Synthesis	The in-itself–for-itself (matter-consciousness)

Source: Sartre, 1984, op. cit., p. 145.

The above relationship is explained below:

> It must be noted here that while the for-itself lacks the in-itself, the in-itself does not lack the for-itself. There is then no reciprocity in the opposition. In a word, the for-itself remains non-essential and contingent relation to the in-itself and it is this non-essentiality which we earlier called its facticity. In addition, the synthesis or value would indeed be a return to thesis, then a return upon itself, but as this is an unrealizable totality, the for-itself is not a moment which can be surpassed. As such its nature approaches much nearer to the "ambiguous" realities of Kierkegaard. Furthermore, we find here a double play of unilateral opposition: the for-itself in one sense lacks the in-itself, which does not lack the for-itself; but in another sense the in-itself lacks its own possibility (or the lacking for-itself) which in this case does not lack the in-itself.[46]

KANT'S INTERPRETATION OF THING IN-ITSELF

According to Kant, "there are things in themselves, which are unknown and unknowable. This doctrine of unknowable follows

[46] Sartre, 1984, op. cit., p. 145 fn.

from his transcendental philosophy".[47] In this context, the following observation is worth noting:

> One of the major problems for Kant's philosophy is the so-called thing in itself. Fichte rejected it. Schopenhauer kept it but reinterpreted it as cosmic will. But we do not know it. Kant says so many things about things in themselves, so how can they be unknown and unknowable? They are ground of appearances and intelligible. Hegel put it most clearly saying, one cannot draw a limit to human knowledge, absolute limit. To set such a limit is already to go beyond it. Kant claimed that we can think about things in themselves, but we cannot know them. In effect, he was making a distinction between thinking and knowing. Thinking involves application of the pure categories. Knowing requires application of the schematized category.[48]

However, the Vedāntist differs from Kant because, "he offers no unknowable 'thing in-itself' beyond phenomena or experience. His reality is experience."[49]

Nothingness

The consciousness as nothingness does not seem to be the lack of reality. This is evident from the following observation:

> If there is to be nothingness of consciousness, there must be a consciousness which has been and which is no more and a witnessing consciousness which poses the nothingness of the first consciousness for a synthesis of recognition. Consciousness is prior to nothingness and "is derived" from being.[50]

It has been mentioned by Sartre that "consciousness is a being, the

[47] Masih, 2002, *A Critical History of Western Philosophy*, p. 335.

[48] Chatterjee et al., 2014, *J.N. Mohanty Lectures on Kant's Critique of Pure Reason*, p. 248.

[49] Woodroffe, 2001, *The World as Power*, p. 196.

[50] Sartre, 1984, op. cit., p. 16.

nature of which is to be conscious of the nothingness of its being".[51] At another place it is stated:

> Negation proper (we are told) is unthinkable; it could appear only on the level of an act of judgement by which I should establish a comparison between the result anticipated and the result obtained. Thus negation would be simply a quality of judgement and the expectation of the questioner would be an expectation of the judgement or response.[52]

Does it mean that negation is just a conceptual entity, it has nothing to do with the reality? This seems to have been reassured by another observation, which states that, "nothingness, the conceptual unity of negative judgements, cannot have the slightest trace of reality, save that which Stoics confer on their 'lection'. Can we accept this concept?"[53] In response to this comment, Sartre has tried to justify nothingness on the basis of interrogative judgement.

In every question, "we stand before a being which we are questioning. Every question presupposes a being who questions and a being which is questioned."[54] This question is a kind of expectation from which a reply is expected from being questioned. The reply will be a "yes" or "no". "It is the existence of these two equally objective and contradictory possibilities which on principle distinguishes the question from affirmation or negation."[55] Therefore, it is always possible to get reply; "Nothing" or "Nobody" or "Never". In that the possibility of negative reply such as "No such a conduct does not exist. This means that we admit to being faced with the transcendent fact of the non-existence of such conduct."[56] Thus, the question is a bridge set up between two non-beings: "the non-being of knowing

---

[51] Sartre, 1984, op. cit., p. 86.

[52] Ibid., p. 37.

[53] Ibid., pp. 37-38.

[54] Ibid., p. 35.

[55] Ibid.

[56] Ibid.

in man, the possibility of non-being of being in transcendent being. Finally, the question implies the existence of a truth."[57]

However, the truth introduces, "a third non-being as determining the question — the non-being of limitation. This triple non-being conditions every question and in particular the metaphysical question."[58] Now the series of questions had led us suddenly that "we are encompassed with nothingness".[59] This explains that, "the permanent possibility of non-being, outside us and within, conditions our questions about being. . . . Being is that and outside of that nothing."[60]

Negation is not only a quality of judgement, but it is a prejudicate attitude. This negation is a relation of being. "The judgement is only one optional of it."[61] However, "prejudicative comprehension of non-being: it is in-itself a relation of being with a non-being, on the basis of the original transcendence: that is, in a relation of being with being".[62]

It is stated that non-being appears at the heart of being. This is explained by the fact that I have an appointment with Pierre at 4 o'clock at the Café, I have reached bit late by a quarter of an hour. I look at the room, the patrons, and I say "He is not here".[63] This is in fact the intuitive apprehension of nothingness. "It serves as foundation for the judgement — Pierre is not here."[64]

ORIGIN OF NOTHINGNESS

The in-itself cannot be the origin of nothingness, because it is full

---

[57] Sartre, 1984, op. cit., p. 36.

[58] Ibid.

[59] Ibid.

[60] Ibid.

[61] Ibid., p. 38.

[62] Ibid., p. 39.

[63] Ibid., pp. 40-41.

[64] Ibid., p. 42.

of positivity. Therefore, the origin of nothingness may be looked for in the for-itself, a human being. It is stated that, "we must recognize that only Being can nihilate itself; however, it comes about, in order to nihilate itself, it must be".[65] This is evident from the following observation:

> Nothingness does not nihilate itself: Nothingness "is nihilated". It follows, therefore, that there must exist a Being (this cannot be the in-itself) of which the property is to nihilate Nothingness, to support it in its being, to sustain it perpetually in its very existence *a being by which nothingness comes to things.*[66]

The being with full positivity should create itself a nothingness or transcendent being, for there would be nothing in Being by which Being could surpass itself towards non-being. The being who nihilates nothingness in its being in connection with its own being. It is further stated:

> The Being by which Nothingness arrives in the world is a being such that in its own Being, the Nothingness of its Being is in question. *The being by which Nothingness comes in the world must be its own Nothingness.*[67]

An ontological characteristic of the Being is required for understanding the origin of nihilation. Every question in essence posits the possibility of negative reply. Every question supposes, that we realize "a nihilating withdrawal in relation to the given, which becomes a simple *representation* fluctuating between being and Nothingness".[68]

NOTHINGNESS AND FREEDOM

In the context of nothingness and freedom, it is observed:

---

[65] Sartre, 1984, op. cit., p. 57.

[66] Ibid.

[67] Ibid., pp. 57-58.

[68] Ibid., p. 58.

> Freedom is precisely the nothingness which is *made-to-be* at the heart of man and which forces human reality to make itself instead of *to be*. As we have seen, for human reality to be is to choose oneself; nothing comes to it either from the outside or from within which it can *receive or accept*. Without any help whatever, it is entirely abandoned to the intolerable necessity of making itself be — down to the slightest detail. Thus, freedom is not a being; it is *the being* of man — i.e. his nothingness of being.[69]

The Cogito

Sartre has started his existentialist theory of consciousness with an appraisal of Descartes's Cartesian cogito –"I think therefore I am". On the basis of this formula, Descartes has deduced the certainty of man's existence from his thought. "But Sartre's maxim — existence, precedes essence may be interpreted as suggesting — I am therefore I think."[70] Sartre, in fact, "believes that man cannot act or think if he does not exist before hand. Consciousness, to him, is only a part of the encompassing structure of existence."[71] It may, however, be noted that the suggested formula of Sartre — I am therefore I think — is in complete agreement with Advaita Vedānta in which it is categorically stated that I am therefore, I think.[72]

The Cartesian cogito has, however, not been accepted by Sartre mainly because it does not provide us the picture of the real consciousness — pure and simple. In this context, it is stated:

> The Cartesian cogito to Sartre is the consciousness of the "second order" or the reflected consciousness. Distinguishing the pure

[69] Sartre, 1984, op. cit., pp. 568-69.

[70] Roy, 2013, op. cit., p. 129. In footnote, Krishna Roy has clarified about his formula. "It should be pointed out here that Sartre himself never explicitly declared that 'I am therefore I think'. It is only an implication of this saying 'existence precedes essence' which may be interpreted as I first exist and then subsequently think of something." – See p. 209, ref. 25.

[71] Ibid., p. 129.

[72] Swami Satprakashananda, 2001, op. cit., p. 83.

> consciousness from the Cartesian one, Sartre makes a distinction between the two phases of consciousness, which he calls the pre-reflective cogito and the Cartesian or reflective cogito.[73]

The cogito is treated by Sartre as reflective consciousness.[74] However, reflection has not been given any kind of primacy over the consciousness reflected on. "It is not reflection which reveals the consciousness reflected-on to itself. Quite the contrary, it is the non-reflective consciousness which renders the reflection possible; there is a pre-reflective cogito which is the condition of the Cartesian cogito."[75] This shows that without pre-reflective consciousness reflective will not take place.

Pre-reflective Consciousness (Non-thetic Consciousness) and Reflective Consciousness (Thetic Consciousness)

PRE-REFLECTIVE CONSCIOUSNESS

The pre-reflective consciousness and non-thetic consciousness are one and the same thing. It is also known as non-positional consciousness. Since "by nature all consciousness is self-consciousness",[76] the pre-reflective consciousness or non-thetic consciousness is also self-consciousness. As regards reflective consciousness, it is also known as thetic consciousness or positional consciousness. However, the main difference between pre-reflective consciousness and reflective consciousness is that in the former there is no ego, whereas the ego only appears in the reflective consciousness.[77] It may be noted that, "unreflected consciousness must be considered as autonomous".[78] This is explained below:

---

[73] Roy, 2013, op. cit., p. 120.

[74] Sartre, 2012, op. cit., p. 10.

[75] Sartre, 1984, op. cit., p. 13.

[76] Ibid., p. xi.

[77] Sartre, 2012, op. cit., p. 12.

[78] Ibid., p. 19.

> All unreflected consciousness, being a non-thetic consciousness of itself, leaves behind it a non-thetic memory that can be consulted. All that is required for this is to try to reconstitute the complete moment in which this unreflected consciousness appeared (and this is, by definition, always possible). For instance, I was just now absorbed in my reading. I am now going to try to remember the circumstances of my reading, my attitude, the lines I was reading. I am thus going to bring back to life not merely those external details but a certain thickness of unreflected consciousness, since it is only by this consciousness that the objects have been perceived, and they remain relative to it. This consciousness is not to be posited as an object of my reflection: quite the opposite, I must direct my attention to the objects I have brought to life, but without losing sight of this consciousness: I must maintain a sort of complicity with it, and draw up an inventory of its content in a non-positional way. The result is not in doubt: while I was reading, there was a consciousness of the book, of the heroes of the book, but then I did not inhibit this consciousness, it was merely consciousness of the object and non-positional consciousness of itself. I can turn these results, grasped athetically, into the object of a thesis and declare: there was no I in the unreflected consciousness. . . . When I run after a tram, when I look at the time, when I become absorbed in the contemplation of portrait, there is no I. There is a consciousness of tram-needing-to-be-caught, etc. a non-positional consciousness of consciousness. In fact, I am then plunged into the world of objects, it is they which constitute the unity of my consciousness, which present themselves with values, attractive and repulsive values, but as for me, I have disappeared. I have annihilated myself. There is no place for me at this level, and this is not the result of some chance, some momentary failure of attention: it stems from the very structure of consciousness.[79]

Sartre's theory of non-egological consciousness as mentioned above, is acceptable to Advaita Vedānta school of Indian philosophy. This is explained below:

---

[79] Sartre, 2012, op. cit., pp. 11-13.

> The view that the ego or "I" which is transcendent to consciousness arises only at the reflective level of consciousness is the echo of the Advaita view which holds that the ego (*ahaṁ*) arises when there is *cidābhāsa*, i.e. consciousness reflected in the internal organ; and this consciousness associated with the internal organ, which alone is capable of reflection, may be characterized in the terminology of Sartre as consciousness of in the second degree.[80]

However, according to Sartre, "ontological proof to be derived not from the reflective cogito but from the pre-reflective being of percipients".[81] This is clarified by the fact that "consciousness is consciousness of something. This means that transcendence is the constitute structure consciousness: that is, that consciousness is born supported by a being which is not itself. This is what we call the ontological proof."[82]

REFLECTIVE CONSCIOUSNESS

Reflective consciousness is positional. In that, "it transcends itself in order to reach an object and it exhausts itself in this positing".[83] It is further explained:

> All that there is of intention in my actual consciousness is directed toward the outside, toward the table; all my judgments or practical activities, all my present inclinations transcend themselves; they aim at the table and are absorbed in it.[84]

UNITY BETWEEN PRE-REFLECTIVE CONSCIOUSNESS AND REFLECTIVE CONSCIOUSNESS

The reflective consciousness cannot be separated from the pre-

---

[80] Balasubramanian, 2004, "Advaita Vedānta on the Problem of Enworlded Subjectivity", p. 87.

[81] Sartre, 1984, op. cit., p. 21.

[82] Ibid., p. 23.

[83] ibid., p. 11.

[84] Ibid.

reflective consciousness. This is evident from the fact that "every positional consciousness of an object is at the same time a non-positional consciousness itself".[85]

It emerges that without pre-reflective (non-thetic, non-positional) consciousness, the reflective (thetic–positional) consciousness is not possible. In such a situation, "it is agreed then that reflection must be united to that which is reflected-on by a bond of being that the reflective consciousness must be the consciousness reflected-on".[86] This reflected-on is pre-reflective (non-thetic, non-positional) consciousness.

The above observations regarding the unity between pre-reflective consciousness and reflective consciousness may be reassured by the fact:

> The pre-reflective and the reflective Cogitos are merely the two different phases of the one and the same consciousness. These are really the two successive stages — one of which necessitates the other. The pre-reflective phase is the pure subjectivity having no objectivity in it, but in so far as intentionality or projection is the essential feature of consciousness, it soon transforms itself into the relative phase. In this reflective phase, consciousness is essentially "of" or about something, it reveals the object or Being in-itself. Consciousness, thus, here, is neither a container nor it insulated; it is in the world.[87]

Possibility of Pure Reflection

It is stated that "reflection remains for the for-itself a permanent possibility, an attempt to recover being".[88] In that, the for-itself which has lost itself outside itself, "attempts to put itself inside its own being. Reflection is a second effort by the for-itself to found

---

[85] Sartre, 1984, op. cit., p. 13.

[86] Ibid., p. 213.

[87] Roy, 2013, op. cit., p. 138.

[88] Sartre, 1984, op. cit., p. 216.

itself; that is, to be for-itself what it is".[89] However, "we must distinguish two kinds of reflection if we wish to grasp the reflective phenomenon in its relations with temporality: reflection can be either pure or impure".[90] Pure reflection is explained below:

> Pure reflection, the simple presence for the reflective for-itself to the for-itself reflected-on, is at once the original form of reflection and its ideal form; it is that on whose foundation impure reflection appears, it is that also which is never first given.[91]

Pure reflection happens to be the reflective to the reflected-on. "Outside of that we should have no means of legitimizing reflection. But the reflective is the reflected-on in complete immanence, although in the form of "not-being in-itself".[92]

However, pure reflection is not an ordinary state of consciousness.[93] It "can be attained only as a result of a modification which it effects on itself".[94] This is explained below:

> One might ask why the I appears on the occasion of the Cogito, if it is performed correctly, is the apprehension of a pure consciousness, without the constitution of a state or an action. The fact is that the I is not necessary here, since it is never the direct unity of consciousness. One can even suppose a consciousness performing a pure reflective act which would present itself to itself as non-personal spontaneity. However, we have to consider the fact that the phenomenological reduction is never perfect.[95]

[89] Sartre, 1984, op. cit., p. 216.

[90] Ibid., pp. 217-18.

[91] Ibid., p. 218.

[92] Ibid.

[93] Medhidhammaporn, 1995, op. cit., p. 34.

[94] Sartre, 1984, op. cit., p. 224.

[95] Sartre, 2012, op. cit., pp. 41-42.

Consciousness and Time

According to Aristotle, "it is impossible that time should exist if consciousness did not".[96] This in a way indicates that the existence of time depends upon the existence of consciousness. It is in conformity with Vedānta, in which time is treated as the object of consciousness. However, according to Krishnamurti, "consciousness is the result of time".[97] Time being an "arrow" moving onwards, it does not know in itself. In fact, it is the consciousness which makes the time into past, present and future. It also ought to be recognized that when consciousness descends in human being, it manifests through mind. In that, it becomes self-consciousness, which knows not only external world, but also knows itself. It may be noted that there is no other entity in the entire universe, which knows itself except self-consciousness existing in human beings. In such a situation, it is difficult to understand how the time can create consciousness as mentioned in the discourses of Krishnamurti. We are presenting here the views of Sartre on consciousness and time because it contains both the views: Vedānta and Krishnamurti. This is evident from the observation that "consciousness is the source of time and time, in turn, transforms consciousness to a temporal consciousness for time is the very propulsive heart of consciousness".[98]

TEMPORALITY OF CONSCIOUSNESS

According to Sartre, consciousness introduces temporality not only in time but also into other things. This is "precisely because, consciousness is temporal".[99] This shows that "temporality is a dimension of human consciousness. He thinks that the being of

---

[96] Balslev, 1999, *A Study of Time in Indian Philosophy*, p. 136.

[97] Krishnamurti, 1992, *Choiceless Awareness*, p. 71.

[98] Thomas, 2004, "Husserlian Foundations of Sartre's Treatment of Time Consciousness", p. 127.

[99] Sartre, 1984, op. cit., p. 29.

human reality is itself time."[100] Sartre has defined temporality as follows:

> Subjective process whereby the for-itself continuously lives its project of nihilating the in-itself. Through temporality the for-itself sets up its own measure for the duration and self-identity of things. Time is not in things but flows over them. The for-itself as what it has been (Past), is a flight (Present) toward what it projects to be (Future).[101]

It has been further explained:

> The for-itself endures in the form of a non-thetic consciousness (of) enduring. But I can feel the time which flows; and apprehend myself as a unity of succession. In this case I am conscious of enduring. This consciousness is thetic and resembles a knowledge just as duration which is temporalized under my regard is roughly like an object of knowledge.[102]

It may be noted that "the reflected-on is profoundly altered by reflection in this sense that it is self-consciousness as the consciousness reflected-on of this or that transcendent phenomenon. The reflected-on knows itself observed."[103] That apart, "the pre-reflective consciousness being temporal, is an 'ekstatic unity', which simultaneously exists in three dimensions of past, present and future".[104] How these three dimensions are related to one another to form their unity is stated below.

THE PAST

If the temporal phenomenon is considered in its totality, it would be possible to see that:

---

[100] Bhadra, 2004, *A Critical Survey of Phenomenology and Existentialism*, p. 362.

[101] Sartre, 1984, op. cit., p. 807.

[102] Ibid., p. 211.

[103] Ibid., p. 214.

[104] Medhidhammaporn, 1995, op. cit., p. 55.

> My past is first of all mine; that is, that it exists as function of a certain being which I am. The past is not nothing; neither is the present, but at its very source, it is bound to a certain present and to a certain future, to both of which it belongs. . . . It is originality the past of this present.[105]

However, the past consciousness is not separated from the present consciousness. This is evident from the fact that:

> The prior consciousness is always there (though with the modification of pastness). It constantly maintains a relation of interpretation with the present consciousness, but on the basis of this existential relation it is put out of the game, out of the circuit, between parentheses.[106]

It is clearly stated that "for human reality alone the existence of a past is manifest because it has been established that human reality has to be what it is. It is through the for-itself that the past arrives in the world because its 'I am' is in the form of an I am me".[107] However, the for-itself is such that, "it has the right to turn back on itself toward its own origin. The being by which the 'Why' comes into being has the right to posit its own 'Why' since it is itself an interrogation, a 'Why'."[108]

The existence of past has been reassured by Sartre. This is evident from the following observation:

> Death reunites us with ourselves. Eternity has changed us into ourselves. At the moment of death we are: that is, we are defenseless before the judgments of others. They can decide in truth what we are: ultimately we have no longer any chance of escape from what an all knowing intelligence could do. . . . By death the for-itself is changed forever into an in-itself in that it has slipped entirely into the past. Thus, the past is the ever-

---

[105] Sartre, 1984, op. cit., p. 163.

[106] Ibid., p. 64.

[107] Ibid., p. 168.

[108] Ibid., p. 788.

growing totality of the in-itself which we are.[109]

Being in-itself is non-conscious Being. "It is the Being of the phenomenon and overflows the knowledge which we have of it. It is plenitude, and strictly speaking we can say of it only that it is."[110]

Sartre says that "My essence is in the past".[111] However, "existence precedes essence".[112]

THE PRESENT

The in-itself is the past. As against this, the present happens to be the for-itself, which is defined here as presence to being.[113] From the for-itself, "the present enters into the world; the beings of the world are co-present, in fact, just in so far as one and the same for itself is at the same time present to all of them".[114] It is further stated that "the for-itself is a witness of itself in the presence of being as not being that being; presence to being is the presence of the for-itself in so far as the for-itself is not".[115] In fact,

> The present is precisely this negation of being, this escape from being inasmuch as being is there as that from which one escapes. The For-itself is present to being in the form of flight: the Present is a perpetual flight in the face of being. Thus, we have precisely defined the fundamental meaning of the Present: the Present is not.[116]

It may, however, be noted that "at present it is not what it is (past) and it is what it is not (future). Here then we are referred to the

---

[109] Sartre, 1984, op. cit., p. 169.

[110] Ibid., p. 800.

[111] Ibid., p. 175.

[112] Ibid., p. 725.

[113] Ibid., p. 177.

[114] Ibid.

[115] Ibid., p. 178.

[116] Ibid., p. 179.

future."[117]

THE FUTURE

The future arrives in the world only through human reality. "The future, like the past, does not exist as a phenomenon of that original temporality of being in-itself".[118] However, the future in terms of consciousness has described in the following observation:

> The For-itself is the thetic consciousness of the world in the form of presence and non-thetic self-consciousness. Thus, what is ordinarily revealed to consciousness is the future world without consciousness being aware that it is the world in so far as it will appear to a consciousness, the world in so far as it is posited as future by the presence of a For-itself to come. This world has meaning as future only in so far as I am present to it as another who I will be, in another position, physical, emotional, social, etc. Yet it is this which is at the end of my present For-itself and beyond being in-itself, and this is the reason why we have a tendency first to present the future as a state of the world and to make it appear subsequently on the ground of the world.[119]

It may be noted that "the future is the ideal point where the sudden infinite comprehension of facticity (past) of the For-itself (present), and of its possible (a particular Future) will at last cause the Self to arise as the existence in-itself of the For-itself. The project of the For-itself toward the future which it is a project toward the in-itself".[120] However, "the future constitutes the meaning my present For-itself, as the project of its possibility".[121]

THE EKSTATIC UNITY OF CONSCIOUSNESS

It is stated that "it is impossible to conceive of a consciousness

---

[117] Sartre, 1984, op. cit., p. 179.

[118] Ibid., p. 180.

[119] Ibid., pp. 183-84.

[120] Ibid., pp. 184-85.

[121] Ibid., p. 185.

which would not exist in these three dimensions".[122] In that, three requirements are to be fulfilled. These are:

i. to not be what it is,
ii. to be what it is not, and
iii. to be what it is not and to not be what it is.

These three requirements are within the unity of a perpetual referring. "Here we are dealing with three ekstatic dimensions: the meaning of the ekstases is distance from self".[123] In this context, it may be stated that "consciousness (in the present) is not what it is (past), it is what it is not (the future)".[124]

It may be noted that "not what is" is used in the sense of past. Whereas it is what it is not is a possibility for future. Consciousness is treated as nothingness by Sartre mainly because everything exists outside of consciousness. In this context, it is observed that "consciousness can exist simultaneously in the three ekstases of past, present and future because at the present it is nothingness".[125]

Concluding Remarks

The reflective consciousness has been explained on the basis of the pre-reflective consciousness. It may, however, be stated that the pre-reflective consciousness and the reflective consciousness are merely two different phases of the one and the same consciousness. In fact, these are really two successive stages — one which necessitates other. There is, therefore, no explanatory gap in the reflective consciousness, which is more or less similar to the phenomenal consciousness.

Sartre has placed the human beings in the unique position which is evident from the fact that consciousness can exist in the three

---

[122] Sartre, 1984, op. cit., p. 196.

[123] Ibid.

[124] Thomas, 2004, op. cit., p. 127.

[125] Medhidhammaporn, 1995, op. cit., p. 61.

ekstases of past, present and future in the human beings because at the present it is nothingness. Since consciousness is treated as nothingness, it has become the absolute reality. According to Sartre, consciousness is nothingness, because everything exists outside of consciousness.

5

Intentionality in East–West Perspective

Introduction

In Western philosophy "consciousness is defined by intentionality. Through intentionality, it transcends itself, it unifies itself by going outside itself".[1] This has been reassured by Edmund Husserl in stating that intentionality has been understood as the consciousness of something.[2] However, according to Searle, "to explain the mystery of intentionality, it appears to the mystery of mental in general".[3] It is further stated that, "in order to understand our lives we have to understand the structure of intentionality".[4] Memories and perceptual experiences are included in intentionality of consciousness. These are possible in waking consciousness under which one experiences of his own action, which is referred to as intentional.

According to Advaita Vedānta of Indian philosophy, consciousness is a waking experience, which is always consciousness of something. In that, "we do not have access to consciousness as such apart from the object which it reveals and to which it is related. When we reflect on our consciousness, we know it to be intentional".[5] This shows that waking consciousness happens to be intentional.

---

1 Sartre, 2012, *The Trascendence of the Ego*, p. 6.

2 Bhadra, 2014, *A Critical Survey of Phenomenology and Existentialism*, p. 65.

3 Searle, 2004, *Mind*, p. 114.

4 Ibid., p. 122.

5 Balasubramanian, 2004, "Advaita Vedānta on the Problem of Enworlded Subjectivity", p. 83.

This chapter attempts to examine the Western phenomenological philosophy of Husserl and Sartre dealing with intentionality of consciousness. This may be comparable to Indian philosophy of Advaita Vedānta which deals with intentionality in waking state of consciousness.

Intentionality of Consciousness in Western Philosophy

INTENTIONALITY OF CONSCIOUSNESS IN PHENOMENOLOGY AND EXISTENTIALISM OF HUSSERL

The concept of intentionality in philosophy was developed by Franz Brentano. who has observed that:

> In perception something is perceived, in judgement something is judged, in an affirmation something is affirmed, in desire something is desired, in hate something is hated. The subjective side of experience of perception, judgement, affirmation, desire, etc. was all that Brentano and after Husserl and other phenomenologists and existentialists were concerned with.[6]

In logical investigations of Husserl, some sort of non-egological conception of consciousness has emerged. "The very nature of consciousness as depicted there was only intentional, i.e. it had as its essential character the projective or directional activity: it was always, consciousness of or about something".[7]

At this stage, it was not necessary to have an ego as basis of the intentional acts. Later on Husserl had changed his ideas in which the transcendental ego has been made ground of intentional acts. "This transcendental ego, for Husserl was consciousness as such, purged of all contingency by the method of epoché."[8] By phenomenological epoché, "I reduce my natural human Ego and my psychical life".[9] The transcendental ego happens to be the phenomenological basis

[6] Sinari, 2007, *The Paradox of Being Human*, p. 49.

[7] Roy, 2013, *Subjectivity in Science*, p. 85.

[8] Ibid., p. 86.

[9] Sartre, 2012, op. cit., p. 55.

and genesis of individual consciousness.[10]

The transcendental ego itself is, however, not "ontologically dependent upon anything else; and, therefore, the only real absolute is the transcendental ego, all else being ontologically dependent on it or relative to it".[11] This is further explained below:

> Only transcendental subjectivity has ontologically the meaning of Absolute Being, that it alone is non-relative, that is, relative only to itself, whereas the real world indeed exists, but in respect to essence is relative to transcendental subjectivity, and in such a way that it can have its meaning as existing reality only as the intentional meaning — product of transcendental subjectivity.[12]

The above observation shows that the ego is not a form-giving subject but a meaning-giving activity. In that, it is the ground of experience. "It constitutes the meaning of the world through its conscious acts. The ego is actual because it lives in consciousness."[13]

Husserl in the ideas says that when he performs the phenomenological epoché (the phenomenological reduction), "the empirical ego and the whole world of the natural attitude are suspended. What remains as residue is the pure experience as act with its own proper essence. And act is found to be related to the transcendental ego."[14] It may be noted that without the reduction, "the apprehension of the ego is not possible. The reduction, therefore, turns out to be the necessary operation which renders pure consciousness accessible to us and subsequently the whole phenomenological region."[15]

What is equally important is that after phenomenological

---

[10] Roy, 2013, op. cit., p. 86.

[11] Medhidhammaporn, 1995, *Sartre's Existentialism and Early Buddhism*, p. 13.

[12] Ibid.

[13] Ibid.

[14] Ibid., p. 14.

[15] Ibid.

reduction, the appearance of the phenomenon of the transcendental ego "discloses it to be closely related to the mystical experience of the inner self, the 'Deeper Self', as Royce called it or the *Ātman* or *Puruṣa* as the Vedānta and Sāṁkhya forms of Hindu philosophy respectively have called it".[16]

As against the above observation, Sartre has denied the existence of transcendental ego. This is evident from the following observation:

> The phenomenological conception of consciousness renders the unifying and individualizing role of the I completely useless. It is, on the contrary, consciousness that renders the unity and personality of my I possible. The transcendental I thus has no *raison d'être*. Indeed, this superfluous I is actually a hindrance. If it existed, it would violently separate consciousness from itself, it would divide it, slicing through each consciousness like an opaque blade. The transcendental I is death of consciousness. The existence of consciousness, indeed, is an absolute, because consciousness is conscious of itself; in other words, the type of existence that consciousness has is that it is consciousness of itself.[17]

It may, further, be clarified here that there is no any room for an I (ego) in unreflective consciousness.[18] This is also known as pre-reflective consciousness. The I only ever appears on the occasion of reflective act.[19] It is stated that "for Sartre does not merely claim that I is a product of reflective consciousness. Audaciously, he tried in addition to demonstrate its absence from unreflective consciousness."[20]

The transcendental ego, "is experienced as the source of

---

[16] Koestenbaum, 1971, "Religion in the Tradition of Phenomenology", p. 185.

[17] Sartre, 2012, op. cit., p. 7.

[18] Ibid., p. 8.

[19] Ibid., p. 16.

[20] Ibid., p. xxi.

consciousness whenever experiencing takes place, that is, whether man is conscious. Anyone can disclose to himself the introspectively verifiable characteristics of the transcendental ego."[21] However, transcendental ego is experienced as distinct from the body and psychical states of the individual. "The I that does the experiencing is structurally different from that which it experiences; the I is the transcendental ego, and the anxiety, joy and body represent the empirical or psychological ego".[22] These two egos create a lot more problem in understanding the different states of ego. The other problem is that how the transcendental ego becomes the source of consciousness. If I am not conscious, where is the transcendental ego. In dreamless sleep, there is no ego, the moment when one awakes, I (ego) starts its operation. This seems to be reason, for denying the existence of ego in pre-reflective consciousness by Sartre. But it also to be recognized that Sartre has accepted the role of ego in reflective consciousness. In fact, the ego becomes the object of consciousness rather than its source. In this context, it may be noted that in Advaita Vedānta entire waking consciousness is treated as intentionality, but it has only relative existence in the sense that it works mainly as external perception under which the objects play an important role.

As regards, the intentional analysis of perception, it also considers other perception. "The material thing is constituted as an objective unity by perceptions which organize themselves into one group. The thing is revealed progressively through the perceptions".[23]

INTENTIONALITY OF CONSCIOUSNESS IN THE PHILOSOPHY OF SARTRE

Consciousness is defined by intentionality. It transcends itself by

---

[21] Koestenbaum, 1971, op. cit., p. 185.

[22] Ibid., p. 186.

[23] Bhadra, 2014, op. cit., p. 73.

going outside itself.[24] It is further observed:

> By intentionality, consciousness is placed in the world, in the midst of life and in direct confrontation with objects. This notion of intentionality, further, has become the source of Sartre's ontological proof, by which he seeks to establish the existence of physical world.[25]

According to Sartre, every action must be intentional. This is explained below:

> Since every action must be intentional; each action must, in fact, have an end and the end in turn is referred to a cause. Such indeed is the unity of the three temporal ekstases: the end or temporalization of my future implies a cause (or motive); that is, it points toward my past, and the present is the upsurge of the act. To speak of an act without a cause is to speak of an act which would lack the intentional structure of every act; and the proponents of free-will by searching for it on the level of the act which is in the process of being performed can only end up by rendering the act absurd. But the determinists in turn are weighing the scale by stopping their investigation with the mere designation of the cause and motive. The essential question in fact lies beyond the complex organization, "cause–intention–act–end"; indeed we ought to ask how a cause (or motive) can be constituted as such.[26]

It is thus evident that actions do have causes but they are of a peculiar kind.

Cause and Motive

Cause and motive are treated as part of the action. This is evident from the fact that "the for-itself must confer on it its value as cause

[24] Sartre, 2012, op. cit., p. 6.

[25] Roy, 2013, op. cit., p. 119.

[26] Sartre, 1984, *Being and Nothingness*, pp. 563-64.

or motive".[27] This is explained below:

> Cause and motive are correlative, exactly as the non-thetic self-consciousness is the ontological correlate of the thetic Consciousness of the object. Just as the consciousness of something is self-consciousness, so the motive is nothing other than the apprehension of the cause in so far as this apprehension is self-consciousness. But it follows obviously that the cause, the motive, and the end are the three indissoluble terms of the thrust of a free and living consciousness, which projects itself toward its possibilities and makes itself defined by these possibilities.[28]

The cause means the reason for the act. One has to provide rational considerations to justify the cause. For instance,"if the government decides on a conversion of government bonds, it will give the causes for its act: the lessening of the national debt, the rehabilitation of the Treasury".[29] However, the cause happens to be objective: "it is the state of contemporary things as it is revealed to consciousness".[30]

The motive is a subjective fact. "It is the ensemble of the desires, emotions and passions which urges me to accomplish a certain act."[31]

UNDETERMINED CHOICE

It is observed that "the cause far from determining the action, appears only in and through the project of an action".[32] This is mainly because the action is defined by intention, i.e. a choice of an end. It may be noted that "the very nature of act as engaged intentionally in non-being would disappear. The motive is

---

[27] Sartre, 1984, op. cit., p. 564.

[28] Ibid., p. 579.

[29] Ibid., p. 575.

[30] Ibid., p. 577.

[31] Ibid., p. 576.

[32] Ibid., p. 578.

understood only by end; that is, by the non-existent."[33] It is, therefore, in itself a negative.

However, "causes and motives have meaning only inside a projected ensemble which is precisely an ensemble of non-existents. And this ensemble is ultimately myself as transcendence, it is 'Me' in so far as I have to be myself outside of myself."[34] This fact is explained as follows:

> I am conscious of the causes, which inspire my action, these causes are already transcendent objects for my consciousness; they are outside. In vain shall I seek to catch hold of them; I escape them by my very existence. I am condemned to exist forever beyond my essence, beyond the causes and motives of my act. I am condemned to be free. This means that no limits to my freedom can be found except freedom itself or if you prefer, that we are not free to cease being free.[35]

The choice is coexistence with consciousness which in a way is the life of human being. In this context, it is stated that "our being is precisely our original choice, the consciousness (of) the choice is identical with self-consciousness which we have. One must be conscious in order to choose, and one must choose in order to be conscious. Choice and consciousness are one and the same thing."[36]

It is further explained that "our actual choice is such that it furnishes us with no motive for making it past by means of a further choice. In fact, it is this original choice which originally creates all causes and all motives which can guide us to partial actions; it is this which arranges the world with its meaning."[37]

In the context of above observations, it is stated that "I am

---

[33] Sartre, 1984, op. cit., p. 564.

[34] Ibid.

[35] Ibid., p. 567.

[36] Ibid., p. 595.

[37] Ibid., p. 598.

referred to myself as well as to my original project; that is, to my being in-the-world in so far as this being is as choice".[38]

Now the problem is how to derive the meanings implied by an act.[39] This may, however, be possible by knowing the source of action. According to Sigmund Freud, the action has reference to the subjects past. This is "the basis of act is in the form of psychophysiological drives."[40] In fact, action is a symbolic manifestation. This is explained as follows:

> To be sure, a particular symbolic act expresses an underlying, contemporaneous desire just as this desire manifests a more profound complex and all this within the unity of a single psychic process; but the complex nonetheless pre-exists its symbolic manifestation. It is the past which has constituted it such as it is and in accordance with classic connections, transfer, condensation, etc. which we find mentioned not only in psychoanalysis but in all attempts at a deterministic reconstruction of the psychic life.[41]

This concept of Freud has been criticized by Sartre on the following grounds:

i. The dimension of the future does not exist in psychoanalysis. "Human reality in the Freudian theory loses one of its ekstases and can be interpreted solely by a regression towards the past from the standpoint of the present."[42] This seems to have ignored the subject, which is signified by its acts.

ii. Freud's theory turns out to be as psychic determinism. In that, "human action cannot be totally free because it is determined

---

[38] Sartre, 1984, op. cit. p. 589.

[39] Ibid.

[40] Ibid., p. 590.

[41] Ibid.

[42] Medhidhammaporn, 1995, op. cit., p. 66.

by the impulses emanating from the unconscious".[43]

Sartre has criticized Freud for giving too much importance to the past dimension of men. He also criticized psychic determination. However, Sartre has conceived the action as turning back of the future towards the present. In this context, it is stated that, "each action manifests the project towards the end in the future".[44] The inferiority complex, for example, "is a project of my own for-itself in the world in the presence of the other. As such it is always transcendence; as such again it is a way of choosing myself."[45] However, "this inferiority which I struggle against and which nevertheless I recognize, this I have chosen from the start. No doubt it is indicated by my various patterns of failure behaviour."[46]

Freud's concept of motivation of action from the past is also not acceptable to Sartre mainly because he thinks that, "the fundamental project, since it is perpetually renewed, is coexistence with the entire life of consciousness".[47]

It may, however, be noted that Freud's theory of psychic determination starting from the past has strong support from Indian philosophy of Vedānta and Buddhism, because both have faith in kārmic dispositions as mentioned earlier. Sartre has not accepted Freud's theory mainly because he has no faith in kārmic dispositions. For him, the one present life is unique. He has no faith in rebirth of human beings. If he would have accepted the past kārmic determination, he would have contradicted his own philosophy.

FREEDOM

According to Sartre, the fundamental condition of all action is

---

[43] Medhidhammaporn, 1995, op. cit., p. 66.

[44] Ibid.

[45] Sartre, 1984, op. cit., p. 591.

[46] Ibid.

[47] Medhidhammaporn, 1995, op. cit., p. 66.

the freedom of the acting being.[48] In fact, freedom itself makes an act. It is stated that, "we ordinarily attain it across the act which it organizes with the causes, motives, and ends which the act implies. But precisely because this act has an essence, it appears to us constituted."[49]

It may, however, be noted that, "if negation comes into this world, through human reality, the latter must be a being who can realize a nihilating rupture with the world and with himself; and we established that the permanent possibility of this rupture is the same as freedom".[50]

In fact, it is the freedom which happens to be the foundation of all essences. This is because, "man reveals intra-mundane essences by surpassing the world toward his own possibilities. But actually the question is of my freedom. Similarly, when I described consciousness. I could not discuss a nature common to certain individuals, but only my particular consciousness, which like my freedom is beyond essence."[51] In this context, the following observation is worth stating:

> I am indeed an existent, who learns his freedom through his acts, but I am also an existent whose individual and unique existence temporalizes itself as freedom. As such I am necessarily a consciousness (of) freedom since nothing exists in consciousness except as the non-thetic consciousness of existing. Thus my freedom is perpetually in question in my being.[52]

The following observations regarding freedom are worth mentioning:

> The conception of freedom, as closely connected with the notion

[48] Sartre, 1984, op. cit., p. 563.

[49] Sartre, 1984, op. cit., p. 565.

[50] Ibid., p. 567.

[51] Ibid., p. 566.

[52] Ibid.

of consciousness, is one of the most distinguishing features of Sartre's philosophy. None of his immediate predecessors held such a novel and exalted opinion about human freedom and its scope. Only Descartes, Sartre believes, gave us the first hint of the notion of freedom as the integral aspect of human consciousness. Freedom, according to Sartre, is unlimited and absolute and this "absolute character of free commitment" lies at the very nature of existentialism. . . . Freedom is inseparable from human being. True to this tradition, Sartre also holds that freedom is identical with conscious human existence. It can never be taken away from a man for freedom is not merely the essence or attribute of man — it is his existence, it is foundation of being — its secret dimension. Man does not possess freedom, man is freedom incarnate. Man, Sartre declares in his *Being and Nothingness*, is condemned to be free. He is free to choose but he is not free not to choose. . . . Sartre shows that freedom is implied in consciousness.[53]

Intentionality of Waking Consciousness in Advaita Vedānta of Indian Philosophy

The mind and senses are active in the waking state, so as to bring the knowledge or awareness of the external world to human beings. In the *Māṇḍūkya Upaniṣad* the waking state has been compared with *vaiśvānara*,[54] which has two words: *vaiśva* and *nara*. The former is related to *viśva*; referred to as cosmic system, whereas the latter (*nara*) is known as individual human. In other words *viśva* pertains to universal (*samaṣṭi*) and *nara* as particular individual (*vyaṣṭi*). "If these two form the two extreme poles of a situation, then *vaiśvānara* is the unitive or non-dual consciousness functioning in the waking state. This life situation forms the *jāgrat* sphere of activity of consciousness." [55]

---

53 Roy, 2013, op. cit., pp. 129-30.

54 Swami Nikhilananda, 2000, *The Māṇḍūkya Upaniṣad with Gauḍapāda's Kārikā and Śaṅkara's Commentary*, v.3, p. 13.

55 Swami Muni Narayana Prasad, 2009b, *Īśavāsya and Māṇḍūkya Upaniṣads*, p. 91.

In the waking state we remain conscious of the external world (*bahiḥ-prajñaḥ*), and the gross objects are being experienced through nineteen facets, which include the five sense organs, the five motor organs, the five forces and the mind, which is known as the *antaḥkaraṇa* in Vedānta. It has four aspects: *manas, buddhi, ahaṁ* and *citta*. So nineteen facets are involved in the wakening state for obtaining the knowledge of the external world.

The peculiarity of the waking state is that it is always mostly outwardly oriented (*bahiḥ-prajñaḥ*). In this context it is stated that, "it remains conscious of everything outside, yet unaware of itself. A subject can know objects while being ignorant of what the subject is. Such is the nature of waking state. All such objects put together form the world (*viśva*); and the individual subject who knows this *viśva* is a human being or *nara*."[56] However, the waking state represents the dynamic modes of pure consciousness, in which the external world and human beings are interacting with each other, so that experience is gained by human beings. In this state, the duality: subject and object is involved in the act of knowledge. Therefore, waking consciousness provides only relative knowledge of things. The experience or knowledge from the external world is possible mainly because human beings have the capacity to perceive the external world.

EXTERNAL PERCEPTION

In the waking state, perception has been given pre-eminence because it provides immediate cognition.[57] Perception is twofold: external and internal. Both are modifications of pure consciousness. Perception by sensory organs such as hearing, sight, touch, taste and smell is external. These sense organs know directly the external world. In the waking state we are mainly concerned with the external perception. However, the mental perception of pain and pleasure of knowledge or ignorance, love, hate, etc. are internal

[56] Swami Muni Narayana Prasad, 2009b, op. cit., p. 92.

[57] Swami Satprakashananda, 2001, *Methods of Knowledge*, p. 36.

perception.[58]

Perception is the direct consciousness of objects obtained through the sense organs.[59] Adhvarindra in his *Vedāntaparibhāṣā* has categorized consciousness into threefold: (i) consciousness is conditioned by the mind; (ii) it is associated with the mental mode; and (iii) it is related to the object. The first is the knower (*pramātṛ*), the second is designated as *pramāṇa* (means of knowledge) and the third happens to be conditioned by the objects is known as *viṣaya*.[60] It may be stated that the perceptuality of objects such as jar is not different from the consciousness associated with subject, i.e. knower.[61] The functioning of consciousness in perceiving the external objects is quite important.

Just like water goes through a channel for irrigating the field, the luminous mind too goes through eye, etc. to the space occupied by the objects like jar, and it gets modified into the form of jar or another object. This very modification of mind is called the mental states or *vṛtti*. Now the consciousness limited to the mental state in the form of jar being in contact with the jar, is not different from the consciousness limited by jar. This is a perception so far as jar is concerned, but not in respect of the qualities or actions in the jar. For perceptions of the qualities and actions, the mental state should of particular form.[62] It is evident that the *vṛtti* theory of Sāṁkhya-Yoga philosophy has been accepted by the Vedānta, although it has been modified.

However, the mind reaches out and assumes the form of external objects, stands in direct conflict with modern Western thought as for example the Cartesian opposition between non-spatial and extended matter, under which "it would be absurd to

---

[58] Swami Satprakashananda, 2001, op. cit., pp. 35-36.

[59] Radhakrishnan, 1999, *Indian Philosophy*, vol. II, p. 488.

[60] Adhvarindra, 2000, *Vedanta Paribhasa*, pp. 13-14.

[61] Ibid., p. 25.

[62] Ibid., pp. 15-16.

assume that the mind is in motion and that it can actively extend out into the space".[63] It may be mentioned that perception in Western thought is based on sensations. This is evident from the observation that "according to most Western thinkers, both realistic and idealistic, sensations are the only direct experience that man has in cognition of an object".[64] Perception as based on sensations has also several limitations which are not generally acknowledged while commenting on the Indian proposition that the mind reaches out to the objects as mentioned earlier. Some observations regarding the limitations of sensation in perception are worth noting.

There is no denying the fact that perception and sensation are related to certain extent. But their differences also ought to be recognized for proper understanding of the role played by the perception in gaining the knowledge of the external world. In a way, perception implies the objective knowledge of external reality through the senses. Whereas sensations represent the subjective feeling of pleasure or pain with which the organic operation is accompanied. This distinction of the objective from the subjective element is important in the act of perception.[65] Although perception and sensation always coexist, the relationship between the two turns out to be inverse to each other.[66]

The inverse relationship between perception and sensation may be explained through the functioning of sense organs. For instance, in the case of sight, it is observed that the objective element is at a maximum. While sensation being the subjective element is here at a minimum; "for in the eye, we experience less organic pleasure or pain from the impressions of its appropriate objects (colours) than we do in any other sense".[67] Therefore, it has been inferred that,

---

[63] Indich, 2000, *Consciousness in Advaita Vedānta*, p. 73.

[64] Swami Satprakashananda, 2001, *Methods of Knowledge*, p. 56.

[65] Bart, 1995, *Philosophy of Knowledge*, vol. II, p. 96.

[66] Ibid., p. 99.

[67] Ibid., p. 100.

"the minimum of sensation infers the maximum of perception; for perception always supposes a certain quantum of sensation; but this is undeniable that above a certain limit perception declines in proportion as sensation rises".[68]

It has been further observed that "ideas which have not their origin in Sensation, come from Reflection. Now reflection is nothing else than an attention to what is in us, and the senses do not inform us of what we already carry with us. This being the case, can it be denied that there is much that is innate in our mind."[69] In view of the above difficulties, it has, however, been asserted that, "the Vedāntic view that mind goes out to meet its object in perception is, therefore, not at all unreasonable, supported as it is by common sense as well as philosophical speculation. The knowledge of external world is explained by this theory for more simply and easily than by any alternative theory."[70] It may also be mentioned that in Vedāntic theory merely taking the mind to the object to assume its form does not explain the knowledge of the object mainly because the mind being the object of consciousness happens to be unconscious. Therefore, the mind has to be associated with pure consciousness (i.e. the *Ātman*) which in turn is observer (*Sākṣin*) of all changes. In this context, it is observed that, "in all empirical experiences the *antaḥkaraṇa* (mind) and the *Ātman* remain identified or fused together, just as in a red-hot iron ball, fire and iron remain indistinguishably blended together. Hence a change of *antaḥkaraṇa* can enjoy the light of the self that is indistinguishably identified with it, and thus, knowledge becomes possible."[71]

MENTAL MODE

There are three different views in Advaita Vedānta as how the

---

[68] Bart, 1995, op. cit., vol. II, p. 102.

[69] Ibid., p. 356.

[70] Datta, 1998, *The Six Ways of Knowing*, p. 56.

[71] Ibid., p. 53.

mental mode (*antaḥkaraṇa vṛtti*) gets united with the external object, leading thereby to its perception.[72] These views are stated below:

i. *Āvaraṇa-bhaṅga* (removal of ignorance hiding the object from the subject);
ii. *Ciduparāga* (tinging the subject-consciousness with the object); and
iii. *Abhedābhivyakti* (unity of consciousness among *pramātṛ-caitanya*, *pramāṇa-caitanya* and *prameya-caitanya.* They become one in consciousness in the sense that the same consciousness gets transformed into three as explained earlier).

It may, however, be stated that in the case of *abhedābhivyakti*, the three functions are just differentiated aspects of pure consciousness reflecting in three different ways.

It is observed that, "this method of *abhedābhivyakti* is open to serious objection. One may say, since the object, a jar for instance, is perceived as non-different from the subject consciousness, why does not the perceiver have such experience as 'I am a jar' or 'In me is a jar' instead of there is a jar."[73] This question can be answered into two ways: (i) fusing state; and (ii) wholeness. Both are discussed as follows. While commenting on the *Yogasūtra* III.3, it is stated.

> Everything in manifestation has two forms. An external form expressing its superficial and non-essential nature which is called *Rūpa* and an internal form which constitutes the very essence or substance of its true nature which is called its *Svarūpa* . . . with the disappearances of the mental *Svarūpa* a faculty higher than the intellect comes into play, and the perception of the reality hidden beyond the object takes place through the instrumentality of this faculty which perceives by becoming one with the object of perception. The perceiver, the object of perception and

[72] Swami Satprakashananda, 2001, op. cit., p. 97.

[73] Ibid., p. 105.

perception become fused in one state.[74]

This shows that perceiver, perceiving and perceived all three become one in consciousness. In other words, the same consciousness gets differentiated into three spheres.

The approach of wholeness is adopted in Buddhism. It is stated below:

> Consciousness has three parts: perceiver, perceived and wholeness. The subject (*darśana-bhāga*) is the first aspect of perception. The second is the object of perception (*nimitta-bhāga*). The third aspect, the base of both subject and object, is wholeness (*svabhāva-bhāga*). Subject and object are born at the same time. When the snail sends up its antennae, he sends up both at the same time. Consciousness can manifest or fail to manifest, depending on whether both the perceiver and the perceived aspects manifest. When consciousness manifests, we say it exists. When it doesn't manifest; we say it does not exist. But this idea of existing and not existing causes us to suffer. The subject of perception manifests at the very moment that the object of perception manifests, and neither is possible[75] without the base. Wholeness is everything.

It is thus evident that in the wholeness of consciousness, perceiver and perceived have no separate existence. One cannot exist without the other.

Now the question arises that if the perceiver, perceiving and perceived are one, why they are treated separately. This may be answered by the fact that the experience happens to be result of the coming together of the subjective and objective sides. In the case of perception, it is only when the integrated state of consciousness is broken into triplicates of perceiver, perceived and perceiving, the individual experience takes place. In this context the following observation is worth noting:

---

[74] Taimni, 1999, *The Science of Yoga*, pp. 282-83.

[75] Hanh, 2008, *Understanding Our Mind*, p. 167.

> In order to understand the nature of experience it is also necessary to remember that the continued existence or maintenance of any mental phenomenon is not possible unless consciousness or the mind is attached to or involved in what is created through the faculty of *buddhi*, the power of perception. It is this essential involvement of consciousness which connects the subject and object and produces experience in all cases.[76]

COGNITIVE PROCESS

It is stated:

> Consciousness is immanent in every phase of existence. While it is hidden in all physical objects, it is manifest more or less in every sentient being. In a human individual it finds expression as distinct self-awareness, which is the only immediate and direct cognition in the strict sense. An object becomes directly known through its association with the immediacy of subject-consciousness. The mental mode brings about the association.[77]

The above statement is further explained by the fact that pure consciousness alone is responsible for the manifestation of all objects (including light).[78] But it is only possible when the veil of ignorance (*ajñāna*), that is the darkness of non-consciousness that hides object before perception is removed.[79]

The mind experiences the external world, but this is possible mainly due to the light of pure consciousness. Therefore, an inference has been drawn that pure consciousness is all that exists. In reflection it becomes many. All differentiations are mainly appearances. In this context it has been observed that "anything we perceive is but a form appearing as an entity because of the underlying reality".[80] This reality is pure consciousness. It has,

---

[76] Taimni, 1998, *The Secret of Self Realization*, p. 38.

[77] Swami Satprakashananda, 2001, op. cit., p. 98.

[78] Ibid., p. 99.

[79] Ibid.

[80] Ibid., p. 84.

however, been asserted that "what we perceive as a chair is pure consciousness apparently limited by the chair form".[81] This has been illustrated by several examples in the following table:

Perceiving Items as Pure Consciousness	*Apparently Limited by**
Chair	Chair form
Fire	Fire form
Heat	Heat form
Sound	Sound form
Ear	Ear form
Mental modifications	Particular mental mode
Happiness	Mental mode to happiness
Mind	Mind form
Cognition	Cognitive mode of mind

*The limiting forms are mere superimpositions and have no existence apart from pure consciousness.

Source: Swami Satprakashananda's *Methods of Knowledge*, op. cit., p. 84.

From the above table it is, however, difficult to understand perceiving the chair as pure consciousness at the first instance. But if one goes deeper into the problem in the Vedāntic framework, it could be easily explained as follows:

> While consciousness, as identical with knowledge, is always conceived to be about some object, *caitanya* as the undifferentiated reality, does not necessarily imply the existence of some object. In its isolated character, it may be described only as self-shining. This characteristic of *caitanya*, in its pure aspect is not altogether absent in the stage of differentiation. It is in virtue of this fundamental quality that an object appears and the subject knows. Appearance and knowledge are but the two differentiated sides of the same neutral fact of immediacy. In other words, the appearance of *caitanya* as object to *caitanya* as subject, or the knowledge on the part of *caitanya* as subject of *caitanya* as object, has to be credited to the fundamental self-manifesting

[81] Swami Satprakashananda, 2001, op. cit., p. 84.

characteristics of *caitanya*.[82]

However, the above observation of perceiving the chair as pure consciousness limited by the form of chair may be supported by two facts: one is based on the Vedic vision, and second is from the Kashmir Śaivism. Both the arguments are stated as follows:

i. When we receive the stimulus from the external world, it forms the image reaching to the sense organ. This in turn gets transformed into the object. In this context it is stated that:

   Transcription of the stimulus into the perceived object is the crucial point of coming together of the subject and the object. Here the source of the stimulus assumes the farm of object perceived through the intermingling of the subjective with the objective. What happens in the event of intermingling is that by way of transcribing the stimulus into the object of perception, it is actually the consciousness which comes to assume the farm of the object which otherwise in itself remains imperceptible to us even after we have the notion of having perceived it. A simple generalization of this process is sure to lead us to the conclusion that whatever we perceive in the external world, apart from what actually it is, is simply a projection of our own consciousness, on that imperceptible and inexplicable something. Though a sheer projection of consciousness, our percept, however, is felt as much existing there outside us in all its material correctness and tangibility.[83]

ii. It is pointed out that:

   The events which constitute the universe are always internal events happening within consciousness because their essential nature is consciousness itself. We can only account for the fact that things appear if there is an

[82] Datta, 1998, op. cit., p. 74.

[83] Singh, 2004, *Vedic Vision of Consciousness and Reality*, p. 15.

> essential identity between consciousness and the object perceived. If physical objects were really totally material, that is, part of a really independent of, and external to, consciousness, it could never be experienced.[84]

Perceptual Illusion

An object like silver perceived can neither be real for, it is sublated by the knowledge of the nacre, nor it can be unreal because it is perceived.[85] Therefore, an object like silver is indefinable (*anirvacanīya*), as existent or non-existent. The theory of *anirvacanīya-khyāti* is advocated by the Advaita Vedānta. It has recently been observed that the theory of *anirvacanīya-kyāti* (i.e. the inexplicability of appearance) in a way is derivable from the Buddhist's view[86] which is nothing but the revelation of awareness itself (*ātma-khyāti*)[87]

However, the illusory object according to the Advaita Vedānta arises from ignorance (*ajñāna*), which happens to be just the opposite of knowledge. It is associated with the substratum being pure consciousness. In fact, pure consciousness underlies each and every phase of existence.

> While it is concealed in all physical objects, it shines as conscious self in sentient beings. . . . An object is perceived when the light of consciousness that shines in a living individual, being manifest in his mental mode conforming to the object, withdraws its veil of *ajñāna* and makes it cognizable.[88]

The object has apparent existence (*prātibhāsika-sattva*), which is distinct from the empirical existence (*vyāvahārika-sattva*). However, "an empirical object exists prior to its being perceived

---

[84] Dyczkwoski, 2006, *The Doctrine of Vibration*, p. 47.

[85] Swami Satprakashananda, 2001, op. cit., p. 133.

[86] Matilal, 1986, *Perception*, p. 90.

[87] Ibid., p. 184.

[88] Swami Satprakashananda, 2001, op. cit., p. 134.

and afterwards, but the illusory lasts as long as its perception lasts. It is coterminous with its cognition."[89]

It seems that illusion is also created by the mind, which functions within the framework of the past. This fact has not been directly acknowledged by the Advaita Vedānta, although it is mentioned that the true nature of object is not perceived because it is veiled by the images created by the mind. However, the fact is that the mind works through the past is clearly mentioned in the *Abhidharma* of Buddhism.[90] Now it is reassuringly told by Krishnamurti that "anything that mind recognizes is already known, therefore it is not new. It is still within the field of thought, of memory and hence mechanistic. So the mind must be in a state where it perceives without the process of recognition."[91]

---

[89] Swami Satprakashananda, 2001, op. cit., p. 133.

[90] Halder, 2001, *Some Psychological Aspects of Early Buddhist Philosophy Based on Abhidharmakoṣa of Vasubandhu*, p. 52.

[91] Krishnamurti, 1992, *Choiceless Awareness*, p. 19.

6

Solution to Mind–Body Problem in East–West Perspective

Introduction

THE mind–body problem arises in the Western philosophy mainly because the mind is treated as synonymous to consciousness. Whereas in Indian philosophy the mind–body problem does not exist at all mainly because the mind is treated as the object of consciousness. It may be mentioned that Searle has also treated consciousness as the first-person ontology. But when the mind is treated as identical to brain, it becomes third-person ontology. As a result, Searle has solved the mind–body problem within the field of consciousness. However, Sartre has adopted a unique approach in the sense that he has defined the body which contains the mind. Further, the body is meant for both: for itself and for others. Therefore, there is no mind–body problem in the existential philosophy of Sartre.

According to the Vedic vision, "consciousness grows out of matter only, when the latter becomes organic".[1] Further, the Vedāntic view point is that "the human mind is a creation of consciousness so as to act as an organ of interconnection between the inner and the outer, the physical and the spiritual, and the individual and the world".[2] If these viewpoints are taken into account, it would be all the more

---

[1] Singh, 2004, *Vedic Vision of Consciousness and Reality*, p. 17.

[2] Ibid., p. 74.

easy to solve the mind–body problem.

Western Philosophy

SEARLE'S SOLUTION TO MIND–BODY PROBLEM

According to Searle, "all conscious states are caused by lower level neuronal processes in the brain".[3] Yet, conscious states being subjective, first-person ontology as a real phenomena cannot be reduced to neurobiological basis, because it is a third-person reduction.[4] This biological naturalism about consciousness provides the germ of a solution to the mind–body problem.[5] Searle has solved the mind–body problem as follows:

> At present, I do not just experience the feelings in my fingertips, the pressure of the shirt against my neck, and the sight of the falling autumn leaves outside, but I experience all of these as part of a single, unified conscious field. Consciousness of the normal, non-pathological kind comes to us with a unified structure. Kant called this unity of the conscious field the transcendental unity of apperception.[6]

It is, thus evident that different experiences arising out of single unified structure of consciousness have been treated as the solution to the mind–body problem by Searle. This solution has been referred to as a simple solution to the traditional mind–body problem.[7] However, the unity of consciousness happens to be the most important solution to the mind–body problem, being the first-person ontology. The other solution to the mind–body problem is that the body is treated as inclusive to the nervous system. This is proposed by Sartre and is discussed below:

---

[3] Searle, 2004, *Mind*, p. 79.

[4] Ibid.

[5] Ibid.

[6] Ibid., p. 95.

[7] Balsys, 2013, *The Enigma of Consciousness*, p. 59.

BODY IN EXISTENTIALISM OF SARTRE

The most interesting part is that Sartre has tried to relate the body with consciousness, though the relation between the two is obscured. This is mainly because body is a living object, "composed of a nervous system, a brain, glands, digestive, respiratory and circulatory organs whose very matter is capsule of being analyzed chemically into atoms of hydrogen, carbon, nitrogen, phosophorus, etc."[8] Whereas consciousness is absolute interiority and is known by a series of reflective acts.[9] It is thus evident that body is objective in nature, whereas consciousness is related to the subjectivity of a man. There is no denying the fact that the body and the mind both happen to be the object of consciousness. This interpretation is Vedāntic.

However, the relation between the body and consciousness becomes further complicated, because according to Sartre, "the discovery of my body as an object is indeed a revelation of its being. But the being which is thus revealed to me is the being of others."[10] It means that the other becomes object for me and I become the object for the other. In that, "people have wanted to link my consciousness of objects to the body of the other".[11] Therefore, the body has to be examined on the basis of ontological grounds: Being for-itself and Being for-others.

The Body as Being For-Itself

The for-itself is not only for both: the body and consciousness but also are in the world. This is explained below:

> Man and the world are relative beings, and the principle of their being is the relation. It follows that the first relation proceeds from human reality to the world. . . . For human reality, to be is

---

[8] Sartre, 1984, *Being and Nothingness*, p. 401.

[9] Ibid.

[10] Ibid., p. 403.

[11] Ibid.

> to-be-there: that is, "there in that chair", "there at that table", "there at the top of that mountain, with these dimensions, this orientation, etc.". It is an ontological necessity. . . . In this sense we could define the body as the contingent from which is assumed by the necessity of my contingency.[12]

It is, further, stated:

> The body is nothing other than for-itself; it is not an in-itself in the for-itself, for in that case it would solidify everything. But it is the fact that the for-itself is not its own foundation, and this fact is expressed by the necessity of existing as an engaged, contingent being among other contingent beings. As such the body is not distinct from the situation of the for-itself since for the for-itself, to exist and to be situated are one and the same: on the other hand the body is identified with the whole world inasmuch as the world is the total situation of the for-itself and the measure of its existence.[13]

Body for-itself is never given which I can know. "It is there everywhere as the surpassed: it exists only so far as I escape it by nihilating myself."[14] The body as a necessary characteristic of the for-itself is explained below:

> The very nature of the for-itself demands that it be a body: that is, that its nihilating escape from being should be made in the form of an engagement in the world. . . . The soul is the body inasmuch as the for-itself is its own individualization.[15]

The subjectivity and the objectivity are combined in the body. It is explained by the scientific experiment. This is stated as:

> The result obtained at the end of the experiment could be only the relating of the two series of objects; those which were revealed

---

[12] Sartre, 1984, op. cit., pp. 407-08.

[13] Ibid., pp. 408-09.

[14] Ibid., p. 409.

[15] Ibid.

> to me during the experiment and those which were revealed to me during the same period to the experimenter. The illumination of the screen belonged to my world: my eyes as objective organs belonged to the world of the experimenter. The connection of these two series was held to be like a bridge between the worlds: under no circumstances could it be a table of correlation between the objective and the subjective.[16]

As always I surpass what is revealed to me toward the possibility which I have to be — "for example, toward that of replying correctly to the experimenter and of enabling the experiment to succeed. Of course these comparisons can give certain objective results".[17]

As regards subjective, it cannot get out of itself. Subjectivity is neither presentative nor representative. "The subjective quality of the Other as object is purely and simply a closed box. Sensation is inside box".[18] Sensation does not correspond to anything which I experience in myself or with regard to the other.[19] Sensation supposes that "man is already in the world since he is provided with sense organs, and it appears in him as pure cessation of his relations with the world".[20] Sensation as pure subjectivity happens to be the basis of my knowledge of the external world.[21] It is further stated:

> If I assume a reflective point of view on my consciousness, I shall encounter my consciousness of this or that thing-in-the-world, not my visual or tactile sense: finally if I can see or touch my sense organs, I have the revelation of pure objects in the world, not if a revealing or constructive activity. Nevertheless the senses are there. There is sight, touch, hearing.[22]

---

[16] Sartre, 1984, op. cit., pp. 411-12.

[17] Ibid., p. 412.

[18] Ibid., p. 415.

[19] Ibid.

[20] Ibid.

[21] Ibid.

[22] Ibid., p. 417.

Everything which has been experienced is indicated as my point of view on the world by the world itself. "All this in so far as I surpass it in the synthetic unity of my being-in-the-world is my body as the necessary condition of the existence of a world and as the contingent realization of this condition."[23] It is further explained as follows:

> The body is the contingent form which is taken up by the necessity of my contingency. We can never apprehend this contingency as such in so far as our body is for us: for we are a choice, and for us, to be is to choose ourselves. Even this disability from which I suffer I have assumed by the very fact that I live; I surpass it toward my own projects, I make of it the necessary obstacle for my being, and I cannot be crippled without choosing myself as crippled. This means that I choose the way in which I constitute my disability (as "unbearable", "humiliating", "to be hidden", "to be revealed to all", "an object of pride", "the justification for my failures", etc.). . . . The body conditions consciousness as pure consciousness of the world, it renders consciousness possible even in its very freedom.[24]

Since I can be nothing without being the consciousness of what I am, the body in some sense must be given to my consciousness.[25] Yet, the body is not for me. This is stated below:

> The body cannot be for me transcendent and known: the spontaneous, unreflective consciousness is no longer the consciousness of the body. It would be best to say, using "exist" as a transitive verb — that consciousness exists its body. Thus the relation between the body-as-point-of view and things is an objective relation, and the relation of consciousness to the body is an existential relation. What do we mean by an existential relation?[26]

---

23 Sartre, 1984, op. cit., p. 432.

24 Ibid.

25 Ibid., p. 433.

26 Ibid., p. 434.

The body belongs to the structure of the non-thetic self-consciousness. Yet we cannot identify it simply with the non-thetic consciousness. This is explained below:

> Non-positional consciousness is consciousness (of the) body as being that which it surmounts and nihilates by making itself consciousness, i.e. as being something which consciousness is without having to be it and which it passes over in order to be what it had to be. In short, consciousness (of) the body is lateral and retrospective: the body is the neglected, the "the passed by in silence". And yet the body is what this consciousness is: it is not even anything except body. The rest is nothingness and silence.[27]

The Body for Others

According to Sartre, body also exists for others. We must now study it in this new ontological perspective. "To study the way in which my body appears to the Other or the way in which the Other's body appears to me amounts to the samething."[28] It is, further, stated:

> The Other first as the one for whom I exist as an object: the re-apprehension of my selfness causes the Other to appear as object in second moment. . . . The other exists for me first and I apprehend him in his body subsequently. The Other's body is for me a secondary structure.[29]

The Other's body is indicated by the round of instrumental-things. This is explained below:

> To be sure, the Other's body is everywhere present in the very indication which instrumental-things give of it since they are revealed as utilized by him and as known by him. This room in which I wait for the master of the house reveals to me in its totality the body of its owner: this easy chair is a chair-where-

[27] Sartre, 1984, op. cit., p. 434.

[28] Ibid., p. 445.

[29] Ibid., pp. 445-46.

> he-sits, this desk is a desk-at-which he writes.[30]

The body of the Other as I encounter it is object for me in the contingent form. This is the necessity of the Other's existence of himself to a race, a class, an environment, etc.[31] However, "the Other's body is then the facticity of transcendence–transcended as it refers to my facticity. . . . The Other is originally given to me as a body in situation."[32] IT is further stated:

> The Other's body is meaningful. Meaning is nothing other than a fixed movement of transcendence. A body is a body as this mass of flesh which it is, is defined by the table which the body looks at, the chair in which it sits, the pavement on which it walks, etc. . . . The body is the totality of meaningful relations to the world. In this sense it is defined also by reference to the air which it breathes, to the water which it drinks, to the food which it eats. The body in fact could not appear without sustaining meaningful relation with the totality of what is.[33]

Again, it is stated:

> Even the study of life in the living person, even vivisection, even the study of life of protoplasm, even embryology or the study of the egg cannot rediscover life; the organ which is observed is living but it is not established in the synthetic entity of a particular life. . . . The Other's body is the facticity of the transcendence–transcended as this facticity is perpetually a birth: that is, as it refers to the indifferent exteriority of an in-itself perpetually surpassed.[34]

The body is the facticity of the transcendence–transcended. Body is in space, it is in the situation and in time, it is freedom as-object. It is further explained as:

---

30 Sartre, 1984, op. cit., p. 448.

31 Ibid., p. 451.

32 Ibid.

33 Ibid., p. 452.

34 Ibid., p. 457.

> The Other's body is always a body-more-than-body; because the Other is given to me totally and without intermediary in the perpetual surpassing of its facticity. But this surpassing does not refer me to a subjectivity: it is the objective fact. . . . The Other's objectivity is his transcendence as transcended. The body is the facticity of this transcendence. But the Other's corporeality and objectivity are strictly inseparable.[35]

THE THIRD ONTOLOGICAL DIMENSION OF THE BODY

It is stated:

> I exist my body: this is its first dimension of being. My body utilized and known by Other: this is its second dimension. But in so far as I am for others, the Other is revealed to me as the subject for whom I am an object. Even there the question, as we have seen, is of my fundamental relation with the Other. I exist therefore for myself as known by the Other — in particular in my very facticity. I exist for myself as a body known by the Other. This is the third ontological dimension of my body.[36]

For the Other, my senses are as this table or as this tree is for me. "They are in the midst of the world: they are in and through the absolute flow of my world toward the Other."[37] Thus:

> The relativity of my senses, which I cannot think abstractly without destroying my world, is at the same time perpetually made present to me through the Other's existence: but it is pure and inapprehensible appresentation. In the same way my body is far me the instrument which I am and which cannot be utilized by any instrument. But to the extent that the Other in the original encounter transcends my being-there toward his possibilities.[38]

However, "the things perceived designate that which I subjectively

---

[35] Sartre, 1984, op. cit., p. 460.

[36] Ibid.

[37] Ibid., p. 462.

[38] Ibid.

exist . . .. The experience of my alienation is made in and through affective structure such as, for example, shyness."[39] This is explained below:

> To "feel oneself blushing" to "feel oneself sweating", etc. are inaccurate expressions which the shy person uses to describe his state: What he really means is that he vividly and constantly conscious of his body not as it is for him but as it is for the Other.[40]

It may be noted that even if the arrangement of sense organs allows us to see the body as it appears to the Other. This is evident from the following observation:

> This appearance of the body as an instrumental-thing is very late in the child; it is in any case later than the consciousness (of) the body proper and of the world as a complex of instrumentality: it is later than the perception of the body of the Other. The child has known for a long time how to grasp, to draw toward himself to push away, and to hold on to something before he first learns to pick up his hand and look at it. . . . Again it is necessary that the child begin the learning process with Other's body. Thus the perception of my body is placed chronologically after the perception of the body of the Other. Considered as it is proper place and time and in its original contingency, this appearance of the body does not seem to be capable of giving rise to new problems. The body is the instrument which I am. It is my facticity of being "in-the-midst-of-the-world" in so far as I surpass this facticity toward my being in the world.[41]

Sartre has concluded by stating that we ought to see the body as, "the necessity of a concrete and contingent existence in the midst of the world".[42] That apart, the fact is that in the existential philosophy of Sartre, there is no mind–body problem. This is mainly because

---

[39] Sartre, 1984, op. cit., p. 462.

[40] Ibid., pp. 462-63.

[41] Ibid., pp. 469-70.

[42] Ibid., p. 470.

the mind is included in the body in-itself of the human being.

Our purpose here is to show that if one takes the existential view of body as profounded by Sartre, there is no body-mind problem at all. But the fact, however, is that some of the Western philosophers who are writing about the body-mind problem are not interested in looking at other's observations under which there is no body-mind problem. It is also ought to be recognized that without taking into account others' views, the solution to the body-mind problem will become all the more difficult.

Now let us see how the mind-body problem has been solved by Sāṁkhya-Yoga school of Indian philosophy.

Indian Philosophy

DUALISTIC PHILOSOPHY OF SĀṀKHYA-YOGA: PURUṢA AND PRAKṚTI

Despite the dualistic philosophy of Sāṁkhya-Yoga, the mind-body problem has been solved mainly because the concept of *guṇa: sattva, rajas* and *tamas* operate in both *prakṛti* and *puruṣa*. Therefore, "the distinctions of subjective and objective, mind/body, thought/ extension simply do not apply".[43] However, before discussing the interaction between *prakṛti* and *puruṣa*, it would be quite useful to know separately, because both are treated as independent and distinct entities in the Sāṁkhya-Yoga system.

Prakṛti

Although *prakṛti* being quite subtle cannot be perceived directly, yet it may be accepted on inferential grounds as science has done with the atom.[44]

Prakṛti happens to be the principle of unconsciousness, works

---

[43] Larson and Bhattachaarya, 1987, *Encyclopedia of Indian Philosophies*, vol. IV, p. 68.

[44] Catalina, 1968, *A Study of the Self*, p. 29.

in association with consciousness. It may reveal consciousness or obscure consciousness. When it is said that *sattva* reveals consciousness, what it meant is that it does so relative to the operation of *tamas*. Consciousness is self-revealing.[45]

However, when *prakṛti* suppresses the revealing factor (*sattva*), "it obscures consciousness and is called *tamas*. But both these actions involve activity and this is the *rajas guṇa*".[46] It thus follows that these factors being the factors of matter and mind are composing the whole universe. These three *guṇas* affect things differently. For instance, *tamas* affects more gross inorganic matter, whereas *sattva guṇa* reveals consciousness in human beings more predominantly as compared to *rajas* and *tamas*. It may, however, be stated that the *guṇas* – *sattva*, *rajas* and *tamas* – never exist separately from one another.[47] *Sattva* and *rajas* predominate in thought and *tamas* and *rajas* do so in the gross matter.[48] In a nutshell, *sattva* is the intelligence stuff of potential consciousness, whereas *rajas* is energy stuff, while *tamas* is the mass stuff.[49]

Puruṣa

Now let us see how the concept of *puruṣa* has been treated in Sāṁkhya–Yoga philosophy. As per Yoga philosophy, *puruṣa* is equated with seer (i.e. *draṣṭā*), which in turn is nothing but pure consciousness. Although it is pure, it appears to see through the mind. It has been emphasized that "*puruṣa* according to the yogic philosophy is the Ultimate Reality hidden behind the phenomenal world in its subjective aspect".[50] However, it has been clearly stated that "not until the last vehicle has been transcended can

---

[45] Woodroffe, 2001, *The World as Power*, p. 208.

[46] Ibid.

[47] Ibid.

[48] Catalina, 1968, op. cit., p. 34.

[49] Ibid., p. 32.

[50] Taimni, 1999, *The Science of Yoga*, pp. 185-86.

consciousness be known in its purity? That is *puruṣa*, the real *draṣṭā*."[51] Similar observation has been made in the *Sāṁkhyakārikā* 19 of Īśvarakṛṣṇa, in which it is stated that *puruṣa* is a pure witness, a neutral spectator and a non-agent.[52]

Puruṣa is also defined negatively as eternal and indivisible "without variableness or shadow of turning" as resting ever in its own pure self-identity. It is deprived even of ideal activity and it becomes just the possibility of a pure consciousness.[53]

However, *puruṣa* is different in each body as mentioned in the commentary on *Sāṁkhyakārika* 18 of Īśvarakṛṣṇa. This is mainly due to diverse modification of three *guṇas*: *sattva*, *rajas* and *tamas*.[54]

Having inferred *puruṣa* on the above grounds, it is stated that *puruṣa* or self may be known immediately in its reflection.[55] Since *puruṣa* is nothing but pure consciousness, it has to reflect mainly through the mind. As a result, the essential nature of pure consciousness (i.e. *puruṣa*) cannot be known so long it identifies with the mind which happens to be the object of consciousness. But it is equally important that *puruṣa* or self cannot experience anything without the mind. This is evident from the following comment:

> That self having been reflected in the mind (*buddhi*) and identified with it, appears to possess knowledge, pleasure, etc. which actually subsist in the mind. He means thereby that it is the reflection of self in the mind which appears to experience pleasure, pain, etc. while, in fact they are modes of mind only. . . . The self appears to take on the characteristics of the mind in which it has reflected. . . . This is what is traditionally known as theory of single reflection.[56]

---

[51] Tamini, 1999, op. cit., p. 187.

[52] Swami Virupakshananda, 2003, *Sāṁkhyakārikā of Īśvarakṛṣṇa*, p. 61.

[53] Radhakrishnan, 1999, *Indian Philosophy*, vol. II, pp. 320-21.

[54] Swami Virupakshananda, 2003, op. cit., p. 59.

[55] Bhattacharyya, 1983, *Studies in Philosophy*, p. 192.

[56] Ram, 1995, *Integral Non-Dualism*, p. 110.

INTERACTION BETWEEN PRAKṚTI AND PURUṢA

Having treated *prakṛti* and *puruṣa* as independent and separate entities in their own ways as discussed above, the Sāṁkhya system arrives at *mahat* as the first evolute of an interaction between the two.[57] This interaction (*saṅghāta*) between *prakṛti* and *puruṣa* has brought *mahat* (i.e. intelligent principle of the universe).[58] From this interaction, the creation starts. *Buddhi* in its turn gives rise to *ahaṁkāra* from which the evolution starts onwards. However, the mutual interaction between *prakṛti* and *puruṣa* is necessary for the reason that *puruṣa* without *prakṛti* is inactive, and *prakṛti* without *puruṣa* is blind.[59] In this context the following observation is the most important:

> *Ātman* or self as the centre of consciousness has come to be associated with matter, which the body is, is the problem of all problems, since any problem, whatever, may eventually be traced back to this problem. The intricacy of the problem is reflected in the Sāṁkhya's solution to it in the form of the relationships between *puruṣa* and *prakṛti* as the ultimate sources of consciousness and matter respectively. The relationship, as conceived here in this system of philosophy, is one of the mirror and the object reflected in it. While *prakṛti* is mirror, *puruṣa* is the object reflected in this mirror. It is owing to the reflection of the *puruṣa* received in the *prakṛti* that the latter appears to be imbued with consciousness resulting in her activation and resurgence of her activity. The recourse to analogy, in place of rational explanation on the part of Kapila, the author of the Sāṁkhya system, indicates the gravity of the problem.[60]

Apart from the interaction between *prakṛti* and *puruṣa*, what is equally important is that the concept *guṇas*: *sattva*, *rajas* and *tamas* – operates in the mind and body also. This is explained below.

---

[57] Singh, 2004, op. cit., p. 75.

[58] Safaya, 1976, *Indian Psychology*, p. 121.

[59] Ibid., p. 100.

[60] Singh, 2004, op. cit., p. 123.

Mind (Manas)

On the basis of *Sāṁkhya-Pravacanasūtram* 2.27, diversity of *manas* is explained as:

> The diversity (of *manas*) is owing to the difference of the transformations of the *guṇas*: as is the case with the (diverse) conditions (of one single man).[61]

The commentary of Bhāṣya on the above *sūtra* is worth stating:

> Just as one self-same man puts on a variety of characters according to the influence of association: being through association with his beloved, a lover; through association with one — indifferent to the world, dispassionate, and through association with some other, something else; so *manas* also, through association with the eye, etc. becomes manifold, by being particularized (or specifically differentiated) with the function of seeing, etc. by reason of its becoming one with the eye, etc. The cause of this diverse modification is "*guṇa*, etc.", that is that the *guṇas*, etc. are capable of various transformation. Such is the meaning.[62]

Body

It is observed that, "in a body at rest, *tamas* is patent, *rajas* is latent and *sattva* is sublatent. So whenever there is disturbance of equilibrium of *guṇas*, manifestations occur."[63]

The above observations are reassuringly to be told that the *guṇas* — *sattva*, *rajas* and *tamas* — is operating not only in *prakṛti* and *puruṣa*, but they equally work in mind and body also. Therefore, it may be categorically stated that the mind–body problem does not exist at all even in the dualistic Sāṁkhya–Yoga philosophy.

---

[61] Sinha, 2013, *The Sāṁkhya Philosophy*, p. 258.

[62] Ibid., pp. 258-59.

[63] Safaya, 1976, op. cit., p. 101.

Theory of Five Kośas of the Taittirīya Upaniṣad

ANNAMAYA-KOŚA (MATTER AND LIFE)

The creatures that dwell on the earth are produced from food. When they are born, they grow by food and at the end, they merged in food. Therefore, it is called the medicine for all.[64] *Annamaya-kośa* is made of the five elements: earth, water, fire, air and ether that constitute the physical world. These elements sustain and nourish particular cells. "The atoms of earth go to form bones, of water — blood, of fire — gastric processes, of air — respiration and of ether — support for all these subsheaths."[65] This shows that subtle elements pervade and sustain the gross ones. These elements should not be confused with the scientific concept of atom.

The gross body of human being is known as *annamaya-kośa* (the sheath of food). It is composed of essence of food and is meant of the enjoyment for the individual soul. It is also observed that happiness is always go together with food. It is further explained as follows:

> The eternal value of food is considered a medicine for all and also as an all-healing medicine. Food can sustain our health and can cause disease as well. It becomes an all-healing medicine for everyone when one's self-existence and the value of food are brought together unitively.[66]

PRĀṆAMAYA-KOŚA (VITAL SHEATH)

The vital force depends on the life of all creatures. Therefore, it is called the life of all.[67] *Prāṇamaya-kośa* keeps the physical sheath engaged in different activities and infuses the life into it. In the absence of vital force, physical body cannot live for a single minute.

Of the preceding physical body (*annamaya-kośa*), the *prāṇamaya-*

---

[64] Swami Gambhirananda, 2004, *Taittirīya Upaniṣad with Commentary of Śaṅkarācārya*, p. 88.

[65] Swami Yogeshwaranand Saraswati, 1987, *Science of Soul*, p. 48.

[66] Swami Muni Narayana Prasad, 2009a, *The Taittirīya Upaniṣad*, p. 106.

[67] Swami Gambhirananda, 2004, op. cit., pp. 92-93.

kośa, becomes indeed the embodied self. Further, as compared with the vital body (*prāṇamaya-kośa*) there is another internal self-constituted by the mind.[68]

Prāṇa-vidyā (knowledge of vital forces) has two aspects: universal and individual. On the universal scale, the air is the point of merger of water, fire, sun and moon. Whereas in the case of the individual, *prāṇa* is the merging point of speech, sight, hearing and making and unmaking of determinations. This is evident from the state of sleep in which speech, sight, etc. are merged into *prāṇa*.[69]

The other characteristic of consciousness is instinct of self-protection. It is formed by the permeation of consciousness in life under the domination of the vital. "This is evident from the instinct of self-preservation being confined to the protection of the vital, that of procreation to the promotion of the vital and that of possession of the feeling of the vital."[70] In this process, the consciousness becomes the source of rebirth. In Buddhism, the self has not been admitted directly, but the consciousness is treated as the medium of rebirth. In the case of Vedānta, it is clearly stated that when the pure consciousness descends in human beings it becomes the *jīvātman*, through which rebirth takes place.

MANOMAYA-KOŚA (MIND SHEATH)

The *jīvātman* always reflects through the mind, which is known as *citta* in Yoga and *antaḥkaraṇa* (inner instrument) in Vedānta. It is stated:

> One part of this inner instrument is somewhat gross, this is the *sūkṣma śarīra* (the subtle or astral body). It has two parts, the first being action-predominating known as *manomaya-kośa* (mind sheath), the second part, which knowledge predominating, is known as *vijñānamaya-kośa* (intellect sheath). But these powers

[68] Swami Gambhirananda, 2004, op. cit., p. 93.

[69] Singh, 2004, op. cit., p. 210.

[70] Ibid., p. 223.

> of knowledge and action do not belong to the sheaths themselves in which they manifest.[71]

The centre from which the power or energy arises is *jīvātman*. This may be explained by the fact that:

> *Jīvātman* is related to *citta* from infinity (rebirth after liberation — *mokṣa*), from the very commencement of each creation in the form *bimba-bimbī-bhāva* (relationship of reflector and reflection), the relationships of owner and owned and *bhogya-bhoktr̥-bhāva* (relationship of enjoyer and the enjoyed). *Citta* is also in contact with *ahaṁkāra* and *jīvātman* takes the work from *ahaṁkāra* at every moment.[72]

In fact, "*citta* can serve as the gateway to pure consciousness",[73] which is referred to as *Ātman*. It is, thus, evident that it is the *citta* which works for the *jīvātman* and becomes the substratum of all the *saṁskāras*, *vāsanās* (dispositions) and *smr̥ti* (memory) in the seed form. In fact, *citta* being in close association with *jīvātman*, has special luminosity and is very active. "It appears to be ever conscious. It is ever generating life force in the form of subtle *prāṇa*. It is the revealer of the nature of *jīvātman*. It is described as *madhyama pariṇāmī* because it is subject to contraction and expansion."[74]

Generally, it is stated that "knowledge is inherent in the mind".[75] This is partially correct in the sense that without reflection of pure consciousness in the mind, it may not be possible to obtain the knowledge of external object. Yet, without the functioning of the mind, neither knowledge nor experience is possible. However, "the mind is regarded primarily as cognitive, and impulses, emotions,

---

[71] Swami Yogeshwaranand Saraswati, 1987, op. cit., p. 92.

[72] Ibid., p. 112.

[73] Singh, 2004, op. cit., p. 78.

[74] Swami Yogeshwaranand Saraswati, 1987, op. cit., p. 111.

[75] Swami Bhajanananda, 2009, "Knowledge and Consciousness", p. 91.

desire, etc. are regarded as forces invading the cognitive faculty".[76]

According to the *Taittirīya Upaniṣad*, of that preceding *prāṇamaya-kośa*, this *manomaya-kośa*, is embodied self; "as compared with this mental body, there is another internal self-constituted by valid knowledge".[77] This internal self is known as *vijñānamaya-kośa.*

Before discussing *vijñānamaya-kośa*, it may be mentioned that according to Vedānta, consciousness (i.e. *cit*, *caitanya*) has two aspects: the immanent and the transcendent. In the above discussion of three *kośa*s "all the types of the knowledge are manifestations of consciousness immanent in matter, in life and in the mind".[78] It may, therefore, be said that immanent consciousness is limited by the body, *prāṇa* (vital) and mind in above three *kośa*s (sheaths). "When the limitations — body, senses and mind — are transcended, one may realize an unlimited, unconditional aspect of consciousness".[79]

VIJÑĀNAMAYA-KOŚA (INTELLECT SHEATH)

Of that preceding *manomaya-kośa* (mental) one, this *vijñānamaya* (cognitive) sheath is embodied self. As compared to the cognitive body, there is another internal self-constituted by the bliss.[80]

Consciousness at the transcendent level becomes an ontological or metaphysical principle as the Ultimate Reality.[81] According to Advaita Vedānta, reality is pure consciousness, which is non-dual without any differentiation. This consciousness is known as *astitva-jñāna* (ontological).

The existence of pure consciousness (*Brahman*) has been supported by the fact that the pure consciousness is the self of

---

[76] Swami Bhajanananda, 2009, op. cit., p. 90.

[77] Swami Gambhirananda, 2004, op. cit., p. 98.

[78] Swami Bhajanananda, 2009, op. cit., p. 91.

[79] Ibid., p. 92.

[80] Swami Gambhirananda, 2004, op. cit., p. 101.

[81] Swami Bhajanananda, 2009, op. cit., p. 92.

all: "for every one feels that his Self exists, and he never felt that I do not exist".[82] The same thing has been said in different words in the commentary on verse III.2.7 of the *Muṇḍaka Upaniṣad*. It is stated that "each is conscious of one's own identity as 'I' the specific consciousness called here *vijñānātma* – which also becomes one with the Imperishable Reality, the Self".[83]

How to attain the transcendental knowledge? Or how to know the knower? In verse 1.1 of the *Kena Upaniṣad* the question is revised as to who is the real agent in the individual? This has been answered in the commentary of verse 1.2 of the same Upaniṣad. In that it is stated:

> There is the Eternal Reality behind the mind, life and senses, the mind of the mind, the life of the life. *Brahman* is not an object, subject to mind, speech and the senses. He who knows it will gain life eternal and not the partial satisfactions of the earthly life. Here in the world of space and time we are always seeking the Beyond, which is above space and time. There, we possess the consciousness that is beyond space and time.[84]

ĀNANDMAYA-KOŚA (BLISS SHEATH)

It is stated that when *citta* (mind) is illumined by the light, it suggests as follows:

> The individual soul undergoes contraction and expansion every moment through infusion of consciousness. Because of contraction and expansion on one hand, there is constant emergence of knowledge and action, and, on the other hand, the individual soul experiences its existence every moment in the form of *asmi* (I am) caused by the process of contraction and expansion. By the ceaseless vision of the reaction of the light of self-reflecting in the mirror of *citta*, there arises an experience of

---

[82] Swami Gambhirananda, 2000, *Brahmasūtrabhāṣya of Śaṅkarācārya*, p. 12.

[83] Swami Muni Narayana Prasad, 1998, *Muṇḍaka Upaniṣad*, p. 122.

[84] Radhakrishnan, 2009, *The Principal Upaniṣads*, p. 581.

supremely *sāttvika* nature in *citta*, which is termed *ānanda* (bliss).[85]

This bliss being endowed with changing attributes should not be confused with the Supreme Bliss of pure consciousness (*Brahman*).[86] It is further stated that "the sheath of bliss, though close to *Ātman* cannot be *Ātman* itself".[87]

The above five sheaths (*kośas*) have solved the body and soul problem. It will be discussed below. However, all these sheaths are basically modifications of the primordial matter (*prakṛti*). They do not possess Absolute Reality.[88] That is why consciousness has to transcend all these sheaths, so as to reach its concentricity being its true nature. In fact, it becomes pure consciousness (*Ātman*), the unchanging Absolute Reality, witnessing all the three states of consciousness: waking, dreaming and sleeping. Further, it is pure consciousness (*Ātman*) that enables one to break the bondage of relative world and attains Supreme Blessedness.[89]

Five Kośas as Solution of Body–Mind Problem

In the *Taittirīya Upaniṣad*, the most important problem of body (matter) and soul (consciousness) has been solved in a unique manner. This may be seen from the following observation:

> If *annamaya* is the body, *prāṇamaya* becomes its soul. If *prāṇamaya* is the body, *manomaya* becomes its soul. If *manomaya* is the body, *vijñānamaya* becomes its soul. If *vijñānamaya* is the body, *ānandamaya* becomes its soul. All these are conditional. We find it impossible to say absolutely which is the body and which is the soul. What we see, instead of a division, there is a hierarchy of entities, one end of which appears to be the body, and the other

[85] Swami Yogeshwaranand Saraswati, 1987, op. cit., p. 230.

[86] Swami Nikhilananda, 2008, *Self Knowledge of Śrī Śaṅkarācārya*, p. 88.

[87] Ibid., p. 89.

[88] Ibid.

[89] Ibid., p. 90.

> end appears to be the soul. The entire range as a whole is neither matter nor mind, but something that transcends both.[90]

Although the above statement seems to be confusing, if one goes deeper into the problem, one may get an interesting insight. In this context, it is observed: The word used here for body is *śarīra*, which means "the perishable form". "The word for soul is *Ātman* which means the imperishable reality that pervades the entire form, just as gold pervades the form of ornament. Here what we see is not the duality of the body and soul, but the unity of imperishable Reality and the perishable form which the former assumes."[91]

However the above five *kośas* of the *Taittirīya Upaniṣad* have been reinterpreted as follows:

> The higher transcends but includes the lower and not vice versa. Thus, life transcends but includes matter; mind transcends but includes life; soul transcends but includes mind, and spirit transcends but includes soul. At that point, however, asymptotic at infinity, we have reached a paradoxical limit; spirit is that which transcends everything and includes everything. Or, in traditional terms, spirit is both completely transcendent to the world and completely immanent in the world — and this is the most notorious (and unavoidable) paradox of spirit.[92]

The implication of above observation regarding the mind-body problem is that when the mind transcends to higher, i.e. *vijñānamaya* which is known as self-consciousness, but it includes the mind along with *prāṇamaya* as the body. In self-consciousness, both the mind and body get united. It may, therefore, be said that the mind-body problem gets resolved in self-consciousness which is embodied in human being.

---

[90] Swami Narayana Muni Prasad, 2009a, op. cit., p. 132.

[91] Ibid.

[92] Swami Jitatmananda, 1993, *Holistic Science and Vedānta*, p. 32.

7

Mental Causation and Inner Sense in East–West Perspective

Introduction

THERE are two faculties of knowledge: (i) the faculty of external perception, and (ii) self-consciousness, which is referred to as internal or reflex perception. In this context, it is stated that "it is impossible to distinguish perception or the other special faculties, from consciousness".[1] Through perception we are aware of the phenomena of the external world, whereas from self-consciousness we apprehend the phenomena of the internal. The objects of external perception is presented to us in space and time, whereas the objects of internal perception are apprehended in time and self. These two conditions (i.e. time and self) are fundamental forms of internal perception or self-consciousness. It may be noted that, "the form or condition of a faculty, is that frame-that setting (if I may so speak), out of which no object can be known. Thus we only know, through self-consciousness, the phenomena of the internal world as modifications of the indivisible ego or conscious unit."[2]

According to Rosenthal, inner sense does not exist as mentioned in the Chapter 1, whereas for Kant, "the only sense of 'inner' is what is presented in the inner sense that means my thoughts, feelings, desires. There is nothing more to be called 'inner'".[3] It has also

---

1 Bart, 1995, *Philosophy of Knowledge*, vol. II, p. 189.

2 Ibid., p. 191.

3 Chatterjee et al., 2014, *J.N. Mohanty Lectures on Kant's Critique of Pure Reason*, p. 246.

been observed that "all thought of something is at the same time self-consciousness failing which it could have no objects".[4] The self-consciousness turns out to be the inner sense. This cannot be denied because in self-consciousness, both inner sense and outer sense become one. This is mainly because the latter is only a manifestation of the former. The outer sense becomes the object of self-consciousness according to Vedānta. Except self-consciousness, there is no any entity that knows in-itself. Therefore, inner sense has also been treated as the mental causation.

It may be stated that the Buddhist monk Diṅnāga's doctrine of self-awareness (i.e. self-consciousness) is reflectively aware of itself. This self-consciousness is a sort of mental perception, which is, "free from conception and construction. It forces itself into non-mediated (non-conceptual) grasp of itself."[5] However, self-awareness has two aspects: object aspect and as well as their "own" aspect.[6] The *ālaya-vijñāna* of Yogācāra Vijñānavāda of Buddhism is also the most important because it is the representation of four *vijñaptis*. These are stated below:

> There are four *vijñaptis* which are called *karma* (actions) from the point of view of agent (*kartr̥*). These are namely: (a) "the *bhajana-vijñapti* (world as representation of consciousness), which is the appearance of the stable outer world. (b) The *āśraya-vijñapti* (substratum as a representation of consciousness), which is the appearance of the moving world — the material reality of the living being — the six senses (*āyatanas*) and their bases. (c) The *ahaṁ iti vijñapti* (self-awareness as a representation of consciousness). This is the introspective, continually operating thought "I am"; and (d) The *viṣaya-vijñapti* (objects as representation of consciousness), which is the appearance of shapes, sounds etc".[7]

---

[4] Merleau-Ponty, 2005, *Phenomenology of Perception*, p. 432.

[5] Matilal, 1986, *Perception,* p. 150.

[6] Ibid.

[7] Sparham and Shotara, 1993, *Ocean of Eloquence*, p. 130.

It is asserted that if there is no *ālaya*, these four actions are impossible.

Internal Perception or Self-Consciousness and Reflection as Explained by Sir William Hamilton Bart

According to Bart, "ideas which have not their origin in sensation come from reflection. Now reflection is nothing else than an attention to what is in us, and the senses do not inform us of what we already carry with us."[8] It is further explained below:

> This being the case, can it be denied that there is much that is innate in our mind, seeing that we are as it were innate, to ourselves, and that there are in us existence, unity, substance, duration, change, action, perception, pleasure, and a thousand other objects of our intellectual notions? These same objects being immediate, and always present to our understanding (although they are not always perceived by reason of our distraction and our wants), why should it be a matter of wonder, if we say that these ideas are innate in us, with all that is dependent on them?[9]

These observations may be summed up on the basis of Vedāntic doctrine that "whatever is in the body (*piṇḍa*) is also in the cosmos (*brahmāṇḍa*)".[10] This means that all the elements of the universe exist in human being.

That apart, the fact, however, remains that it is through the faculty of self-consciousness, it is possible for us to have knowledge of the phenomena of our minds. It is the source of internal experience.[11] The critical analysis is limited to the objects of our internal observation. The phenomena of mind alone may be conscious of absolute necessity. "All necessity is, infact, to us subjective: for a thing is conceived impossible only as we are unable

[8] Bart, 1995, op. cit., vol. II, p. 356.

[9] Ibid.

[10] Tilak, 2000, *Gita-Rahasya*, p. 200.

[11] Bart, 1995, op. cit., vol. II, p. 192.

to construe it in thought."[12] Further, it is not possible that "a thing can began to be without a cause."[13] This is mainly due to the fact that "mind cannot realize to itself the conception of absolute commencement."[14] It is further explained as follows:

> Perception, Thinking, Doubting, Believing, Reasoning, Knowing, Willing, and all the different actings of our own minds, which we being conscious of, and observing in ourselves, do from these receive into our understandings, ideas as distinct as we do from bodies affecting our senses. This source of ideas every man has wholly in himself; and though it be not sense, as having nothing to do with external objects, yet it is very like it, and might properly enough to be called Internal Sense. But as I call the other Sensation, so I call this Reflection; the ideas it affords being such only as the mind gets by reflecting on its own operations within itself.[15]

MEMORY

Memory is treated as the conservative faculty by Bart. But, "without a power of acquisition, a power conservation could not be exerted; and without the latter, the former could be frustrated, for we should lose as fast we acquired".[16] However, the fact is that, "memory principally and properly denotes the power of the mind possesses of retaining hold of the knowledge it has required, is generally admitted by philosophers".[17]

It is observed that the knowledge which we acquired is retained in and by the mind. This in a way establishes the fact of memory.[18]

---

[12] Bart, 1995, op. cit., vol. II, p. 194.

[13] Ibid.

[14] Ibid.

[15] Ibid., p. 198.

[16] Ibid., p. 205.

[17] ibid., pp. 206-07.

[18] Ibid., p. 210.

The knowledge that we have acquired by perception and self-consciousness does continue to endure in the mind until it get annihilated by other causes. This is explained below:

> This would in fact be the case, where the mind merely passive in the impression it receives: for it is a universal law of nature, that every effect endures as long as it is not modified or opposed by any other effect. But the mental activity, the act of knowledge, of which I now speak, is more than this: it is an energy of self-active power of a subject one and indivisible; consequently a part of the ego must be detached or annihilated, if a cognition once existent be again extinguished. Hence it is, that the problem most difficult of solution is not, how a mental activity endures, but how it ever vanishes . . . our internal activities in a ceaseless vicissitude of manifestation and disappearance. This apparent contradictions, therefore, demands solution.[19]

The solution to the above problem has been provided in "the theory of obscure or latent modifications: that is, mental activities, real but beyond the sphere of consciousness".[20] However, "the disappearance of internal energies from the view of internal perception does not warrant the conclusion that they no longer exist for we are not always conscious of all the mental energies, whose existence cannot be disallowed".[21] In this context, the following observation is worth stating:

> We take note of our memory only in its influence on our consciousness: and, in general; do not consider that the immense proportion of our intellectual possessions consists of our delitescent cognitions. All the cognitions which we possess or have possessed, still remain to us — the whole complement of all our knowledge still lies in our memory; but as new acquisitions are continually pressing in upon the old, and continually taking place along with them among the modifications of the ego, the

[19] Bart, 1995, op. cit., vol. II, pp. 211-12.

[20] Ibid., p. 212.

[21] Ibid., pp. 212-13.

> old cognitions, unless from time to time refreshed and brought forward, are driven back, and become gradually fainter and more obscure. This obscuration, is not, however, to be conceived as an obliteration, and as a total annihilation.[22]

It may, however, be noted that all mental activities, all acts of knowledge which persist, we never lose them but become obscure. "The obscure cognition may exist simply out of consciousness, so that it can be recalled by a common act of reminiscence."[23]

Inner Sense

The representative theory of perception indicates that everything happens as inner episode within the mind. Now question arises that whether it is possible for everything to happen without any influence from outside. The inner happening in the mind is quite often being justified by the dream experience in which action also takes place. But the fact, however, remains that the consciousness of waking state gives rise to dream-infusing consciousness.[24] Further, it is not possible to separate inside from outside. "Inside and outside are inseparable. The world is wholly inside and I am wholly outside myself. When I perceive this table, the perception of the top must not overlook that of legs, otherwise the object would be thrown out of joint."[25]

However, the similar thing has been observed by Kant in his *Refutation of Idealism*. It is stated that:

> Inner perception is impossible without outer perception, that the world, as a collection of connected phenomena, is anticipated in the consciousness of my unity, and is the means, whereby I come into being as a consciousness. What distinguishes intentionality from the Kantian relation to a possible object is that unity of

---

[22] Bart, 1995, op. cit., vol. II, p. 213.

[23] Ibid., p. 215.

[24] Swami Yogindrananda, 2005, *Pramāṇavārtikam* of *Dharmakīrti*, vol. II, p. 860.

[25] Merleau-Ponty, 2005, op. cit., p. 474.

> the world before being posited by knowledge in a specific act of identification, is lived as readymade or already there. Kant himself shows in the critique of judgement that there exists a unity of the imagination and the understanding and a unity of subjects before the object, and that, in experiencing the beautiful, for example, I am aware of a harmony between sensation and concept, between myself and others, which is itself without any concept.[26]

Self-Consciousness and Mental Perception

Diṅnāga has evolved the doctrine of self-awareness (i.e. self-consciousness), which is reflexively aware of itself. The self-awareness is generally used as a sort of mental perception.[27] Dharmakīrti in his *Nyāyabindu* has clearly stated that *citta* (consciousness) and *caita* (mental phenomenon such as pleasure, anger, etc.) are self-aware.[28] It is further explained as follows:

> Self-awareness is a kind of perception because it is a mental perception that is entirely free from conception and construction. It forces itself into a non-mediated (non-conceptual) grasp of itself. It is called "mental" or "inner" because the external sense faculties are not directly responsible for such a non-mediated grasp of itself.[29]

It has, however, been pointed out by Diṅnāga that cognitive event has two aspects: the object aspect and the cognizing aspect, which are known as the forms of comprehensible (*grāhya*) and the comprehension (*grāhaka*). But there is also another form of self-consciousness in which both forms, comprehensible and comprehension, are revealed. Similar observation has been made by Dharmakīrti also.

---

[26] Merleau-Ponty, 2005, op. cit., p. xix, Preface.

[27] Matilal, 1986, op. cit., p. 149.

[28] Ibid., p. 150.

[29] Ibid.

The position of Dharmakīrti on perception in supporting the self-awareness is summed up very well in the following observation:

> Dharmakīrti's arguments to support "self-awareness" are essentially tied to the Yogācāra thesis that the distinction between the *grāhya* (apprehensible object) and the *grāhaka* (apprehensing cognition) is an illusion like that of double vision of the moon. An awareness event is an indivisible whole, it illuminates itself, for there is nothing else, the two appearances, the object form and the apprehension form, being illusorily created. The non-difference of the apprehensible object and the apprehending subject (the cognition itself) is established by the *hetu*, i.e. on the evidence that these two are always invariably and necessarily apprehended together. Hence their difference is only a convenient myth, a matter of convention only. The self-cognition of a cognition is established because even the perception of an object cannot be otherwise established for him who does not have the perception of that perception.[30]

Self-consciousness has, however, been interpreted as *jīvātman* in Vedānta. It is stated that pure consciousness (i.e. *Brahman*) is manifesting in every human being as self-consciousness. That is, direct and intuitive.[31] This has been explained in the introduction.

The above description of self-consciousness as *jīvātman* is fairly comparable to self-awareness (self-consciousness) treated as mental perception by Diṅnāga. In this case comprehension aspect of self-consciousness happens to be knowing subject, representing thereby as self in perception. This may be reassured by any other observation that "self-consciousness is essentially a case of knowledge, it makes present to us our own self. It is not a construction, it is not an illusion and therefore it is direct knowledge."[32] It has also been assured that without the doctrine of self-consciousness (i.e. self-cognition) recollection is not possible.

---

[30] Matilal, 1986, op. cit., p. 154.

[31] Swami Satprakashananda, 2001, *Methods of Knowledge*, p. 91.

[32] Stcherbatsky, 1996, op. cit., vol. II, p. 30.

Ālaya-Vijñāna and Karmic Seed in Yogācāra Vijñānavāda Buddhism

ĀLAYA-VIJÑĀNA: FACTORS RESPONSIBLE FOR ITS ORIGIN

The idea of a causal seed of the Sautrāntikas and consciousness continuum vaguely present in the *bhavaṅga citta,* seem to have contributed to the development of the notion of *ālaya-vijñāna* in the Yogācāra Vijñānavāda.[33] It is capable of holding and retaining the seeds of all *dharmas*, which are not present in any other consciousness.[34] However, the *ālaya-vījñāna* has been introduced to explain several unconscious states. This is evident from the following observations:

> Where the Buddhist faced the problem of explaining the causal continuity between the immediately preceding *vijñāna,* "consciousness moment" and the new "waking" *vijñāna* following such a state. For example there may be a (i) seizure or swoon (*mūrcchā*) or (ii) a state of extreme inaction (*middha*) or, there may be (iii) meditational cessation of the ego-shrunk mind stream or (iv) some other higher-order meditational cessation (cf. *nirodha-samāpatti*, etc.). . . . In the Yogācāra system, however, with the introduction of *ālaya-vijñāna,* it was easy to explain the causal sequence satisfactorily. The flow of *ālaya-vijñāna* continues in all the above-mentioned states.[35]

KĀRMIC SEED

The *ālaya-vijñāna* contains the seeds or impressions (*vāsanās*) of whatsoever *karma* has been performed whether it is good, bad or indifferent.[36] According to the *Laṅkāvatārasūtra* based on the commentary of Zen Buddhism, *vāsanā* (disposition) is explained as follows:

---

[33] Matilal, 1997, *Logic, Language and Reality*, p. 337.

[34] Ganguly, 1992, *Treatise in Thirty Verses on Mere Consciousness*, p. 79.

[35] Matilal, 1997, op. cit., p. 339.

[36] Chatterjee, 1999, *The Yogācāra Idealism*, p. 88.

> In the sense a perfuming energy that leaves its essence permanently behind in the things it has perfumed . . . *vāsanā*, therefore, is a kind of supersensous energy mysteriously emanating from every thought, feeling or every deed one has done or does, which lives latently in the storehouse called *ālaya-vijñāna*. . . . In modern psychology we can say that *vāsanā* corresponds to memory in its widest sense. This perfuming or leaving impressions is sometimes known as sowing seeds (*bīja*).[37]

The *ālaya-vijñāna* is called *vipāka*, because it is the fruit of past *vāsanās* (impressions), which are of two kinds, viz. (i) *vipāka vāsanā*, and (ii) *niṣyanda vāsanā*. According to the *Laṅkāvatārasūtra*,

> By *vipāka* effect is meant that the nature of an effect is not the same as the nature of the cause. . . . But there is an intimate relationship between them as cause and effect. In the case of the *niṣyanda*, however, cause and effect are of similar nature. An act of goodness tends to produce the disposition to more good; an effect of the same quality flows of its cause.[38]

This shows that *vipāka* and *niṣyanda* are expressing different forms of effect that flows out its cause. However, the *vipāka vāsanā* is interpreted in clear terms as a stream of mental process, i.e. the continuity of the individual through the successive births, whereas *niṣyanda* is the purification of the present experiences. "*Vipāka vāsanā* maintains the cycle of births; *niṣyanda vāsanā* supplies the content of each birth."[39]

The *bījas* (kārmic seeds) have seven characteristics:

i. the *bījas* are momentary (*kṣaṇika*): they perish immediately after birth but possess the power of activity;
ii. *bīja* is the *dharma* which is actually connected with its fruit;
iii. the *bījas* continue in a homogeneous uninterrupted series

---

[37] Suzuki, 1999, *Studies in the Laṅkāvatārasūtra*, pp. 178-79.

[38] Ibid., p. 323.

[39] Chatterjee, 1999, op. cit., p. 89.

until the final stage of the holy path of ascetic practices is attained,

iv. the *bījas* have the capacity to produce actual *dharmas* – good, bad or non-defined, which have perfumed and created them;

v. the *bījas* depend on a group of conditions to produce the actual *dharma*;

vi. each *bīja* produces its own fruit; and

vii. A *bīja* of *citta* leads to the manifestation of *citta.*[40]

MAIN FUNCTION OF VIJÑĀNA, FLOW AND INTERNAL CAUSATION

Main Function

According to the Zen Buddhism's commentary on the *Laṅkāvatārasūtra*, the main function of the *ālaya-vijñāna* is to look into itself where all the *vāsanās* (memory) are preserved from the beginningless past. It is always ready for further evolution, but the main problem is that it has no active energy in itself to act. It simply perceives. In that, it looks like an ocean with no waves disturbing its tranquillity. In such a situation the *ālaya-vijñāna* in itself is free from a dualism of subject and object and differentiation. However, the waves will be seen in the ocean of *ālaya-vijñāna* "when the principle of individuation known as *viṣaya* blows over it like the wind. The waves thus started are the world of particulars, where the intellect discriminates the affection clings and passions and desires struggle for existence and supremacy".[41]

The *ālaya-vijñāna* manifests through *manas*. However, "the function of *manas* is essentially to reflect upon the *ālaya* and to create and to discriminate subject and object from the pure oneness of the *ālaya*. The memory accumulated (*ciyate*) in the latter is now divided (*viciyate*) into dualities of all forms and all kinds. This is compared to the manifoldness of waves that stir

[40] Ganguly, 1992, op. cit., pp. 40-41.

[41] Suzuki, 1999, op. cit., p. 190.

up the ocean of the *ālaya*."[42] In fact, it is the *manas* (mind) which creates the duality of subject and object out of the absolute unity of the *ālaya*.[43]

FLOW OF ĀLAYA-VIJÑĀNA

The *ālaya-vijñāna* being the stream of consciousness "it is neither permanent nor impermanent". According to Vasubandhu, this consciousness has evolved in a homogeneous series without interruption from beginningless time. In that it becomes perpetual evolution like a violent torrent.[44] It may be stated that the *ālaya-vijñāna* as cause it is perished and as effect it is born from one moment to another. "Because the effects are born it is not impermanent. Because the causes are perished, it is not permanent."[45]

The *ālaya-vijñāna* as stream of consciousness gets arrested in the state of *arhat*. "In this state one is completely cut off from the obstruction of defilements and thus goes beyond the possibility of rebirth."[46]

INTERNAL CAUSATION

The various *dharmas* are developed from the *ālaya* as its image aspect (*nimitta-bhāga*) under which the *ālaya* has its object (*ālambana*). In relation to this object, it has its mode of activity (*ākāra*), i.e. perception. This happens to be the perception aspect (*darśana-bhāga*) of the *ālaya-vijñāna*. The *darśana-bhāga* is quite subtle and very difficult to perceive. It may, however, be noted that the *nimitta-bhāga* of *ālaya* is also subtle because the internal objects of the *bījas* and sense organs are extremely subtle. Whereas

---

[42] Suzuki, 1999, op. cit., p. 190.

[43] Ibid., p. 191.

[44] Ganguly, 1992, op. cit., p. 42.

[45] Ibid.

[46] Ibid.

the external objects of *bhajanaloka* is immeasurable.[47] Therefore, in the *ālaya-vijñāna* the whole operation happens to be the internal causation. Thus "there is no external causation; but because of the various evolutions or developments (*pariṇāma*) of the *bījas* in the *ālaya-vijñāna*, and by the force of mutual assistance of the actual eight consciousnesses, such and such types of distinctions are produced".[48]

Now question arises, if the *ālaya-vijñāna* exists due to internal causation without any external forces, how does the distinction (*vikalpa*), the transformation of consciousness into the *darśana-bhāga* (subjective) and the *nimitta-bhāga* (objective) take place. In this context, it is stated that the *vikalpas* (subject and object distinction) are born because the kārmic seeds (*bījas*) and the *dharmas* work as conditions (*pratyayas*). Let us see how these conditions are comprehended?

FOUR PRATYAYAS

1. *Hetu-pratyaya*: It refers to the conditioned (*saṁskṛta*) *dharmas*, which produce their fruit immediately. However, "the *bījas* are *hetu-pratyaya* in double action: on the one hand, they lead to the production of *bījas* of the same species subsequently. On the other hand, they produce actual consciousness of the same species simultaneously."[49]

In the *Abhidharmakośa* except *kāraṇa-hetu*, there are five *hetu-pratyayas*. These are *sahabhū-hetu*, *samprayuktaka-hetu*, *sabhāga-hetu*, *sarvatraga-hetu* and *vipāka-hetu*. Out of five, the most important in the present context is *sabhāga-hetu* which is discussed below:

Sabhāga-hetu: It is defined as homogeneity. The cause is always antecedent to the effect. This is applicable to all *dharmas* of the same

---

[47] Ganguly, 1992, op. cit., p. 41.

[48] Ibid., p. 116.

[49] Ibid., p. 49.

category.[50] *Sabhāgatā* indicates a feature of likeness or homogeneity among human beings. It is found in every human being. However, "according to the Sautrāntikas, *sabhāgatā* is not *dravyasat* (real)".[51] The following observation is worth noting:

> *Sabhāgatā* indicates the abstract basis of personality phenomenon or uniqueness of *astitva* in general. This view seems to be supported by *koṣa* which holds that *sabhāgatā* in a sense forms the abstract and subtle potentiality of an individual. *Saṁskāra* of *sabhāgatā*, thus, accounts for an individual's uniqueness. *Sabhāgatā* links up the moments after moments of existence (*bhāva*), extending over the different cycles of birth and death. *Sabhāgatā* may be interpreted then both as the potentiality and manifestation of entire *bhāva* or existence which is only disrupted at the time of *nirvāṇa*. . . . *Sabhāgatā* as a *citta viprayukta dharma* may be similarly understood as a substratum of individual's life (*jīvita*) functioning along with mind (*citta*).[52]

2. *Samānāntara-pratyaya*: In the stream of thought every preceding moment of consciousness becomes the cause of the succeeding moment. This gives rise to a momentary homogeneous series, representing thereby the life continuum. In this context it is observed that "*samānāntara-pratyaya* is now replaced by the relation of the stored-consciousness (*ālaya*) to its modification (*pariṇāma*)".[53]

The *ālaya-vijñāna* is here a storehouse where the kārmic seeds (*bīja*) in the form of impressions (*vāsanā*) are stored up. This is evident from the following observation:

> It belongs to the phenomenal part of existence because all the results (*vipāka*) of *karma* are there stored up. This store-consciousness in this system occupies a position analogous to the

[50] Chaudhury, 1983, *Analytical Study of the Abhidharmakośa*, p. 111.

[51] Haldar, 2001, *Some Psychological Aspects of Early Buddhist Philosophy Based on Abhidharmakośa of Vasubandhu*, p. 125.

[52] Ibid., pp. 126-27.

[53] Stcherbatsky, 2003, *The Conception of Buddhist Nirvana*, p. 38.

primitive matter (*pradhāna*) of the Sāṁkhya school. All individual objects and ideas are regarded as its modifications (*pariṇāma*) by the Sāṁkhya. The Yogācāras likewise regard all separate ideas as modifications of their store-consciousness. This represents a disguised return from the theory of a stream of thought to the doctrine of substantial soul.[54]

3. ***Ālambana-pratyaya*:** It is the relation between the object and the subject of perception. All the *dharmas* constituted and unconstituted (*saṁskṛta* and *asaṁskṛta*) function as the *ālambana-pratyaya* of the mind and mental states (*citta-caitta*).[55]

4. ***Adhipati-pratyaya*:** "It is real *dharma* (*saddharma*, conditioned or unconditioned as opposed to *parikalpita-svabhāva*) possessing potent energy and capable of promoting or counteracting the development of another *dharma*."[56]

In the manifestation of *ālaya-vijñāna*, all the above causes are required. This is evident from the fact that "the cause as condition (*hetu-pratyaya*) is the seed from which things arise, but nothing can arise from this alone. There also has to be a development condition (*adhipati-pratyaya*), an object condition (*ālambana-pratyaya*), and the condition of immediate continuity (*samānāntara-pratyaya*)."[57]

FIVE MENTAL FACTORS ASSOCIATED WITH ĀLAYA-VIJÑĀNA

The *ālaya-vijñāna* from beginningless time up to the realization of *nirvāṇa* is associated in all states with five *caittas*: *sparśa*, *manaskāra*, *vedanā*, *saṁjñā* and *cetanā*. These factors known as universal (*sarvatraga*) are discussed below.

Sparśa (Mental Contact)

The mental contact takes place in conjunction with three things:

---

54 Stcherbatsky, 2003, op. cit., pp. 37-38.

55 Chaudhury, 1983, op. cit., p. 114.

56 Ganguly, 1992, op. cit., p. 50.

57 Hanh, 2008, *Understanding Our Mind*, p. 102.

occurrence of consciousness, sense faculty and object. These factors work in conjunction as follows:

> It acts like a basis for sensation (*vedanā*), conception (*saṁjñā*), volition (*cetanā*), etc. The triad consists of sense organ (*indriya*), the object (*viṣaya*) and the consciousness (*vijñāna*) and when the union takes place as a result of their mutual coordination (like the union of eye, form and visual consciousness and not the union of ear, odour and auditory consciousness), it is called the tripartite conjunction (*trika-sannipāta*). These three pre-exist in the state of *bījas*. The *sparśa* which also pre-exists in the state of the *bījas* is based on these three to be reborn. When it is reborn, it causes three to be united.[58]

However before union, these three factors do not have the power to produce the *citta-caittas*. They acquire the power at the moment of their union.[59]

Vedanā (Sensation)

Sensation is the mental factor that experiences the characteristics of an object, whether it is agreeable or disagreeable. The activity of *vedanā* produces a craving, because it has a desire for union (*saṁyoga*) or separation (*viyoga*) or neither union or separation.[60]

The agreeable characteristics of an object produces the experience of joyful sensation. Whereas disagreeable characteristics of object gives rise to sorrowful sensation. The experience of neutral characteristics is giving the sensation neither joyful nor sorrowful.[61]

Saṁjñā (Conception)

The nature of conception determines the characteristics of an object. Further, the mental activity of conception produces the

---

[58] Ganguly, 1992, op. cit., p. 82.

[59] Ibid.

[60] Ibid., p. 83.

[61] Ibid.

various names and concepts. "When the characteristics of an object is established (*vyavasthita*), this is blue, not blue, only then various expressions that correspond to general characteristics can be produced."[62]

Manaskāra (Attention)

Attention is the mental factor responsible for the mind's advertence to the object by which it gets presented to consciousness. In fact, attention by and large is responsible for the cognitive factor in all states of consciousness. However, in the case of *ālaya-vijñāna* attention excites, "the *bījas* of the mind which about to be born, and directs this mind once born, in such a manner that it is fixed on the object".[63]

Cetanā (Volition)

The Buddha has declared that volition is *karma*. Having willed, one acts by body, by speech and by thought.[64] The *cetanā* (volition) while conditioning the mind, so as to create and act; its activity is to manoeuvre the mind to act in such a way that it produces good, etc.[65]

SENSATION OF ĀLAYA-VIJÑĀNA

The nature of *ālaya-vijñāna* and two sensations of joy and suffering are quite different, because the mode of activity (*akāra*) of *ālaya-vijñāna* is quite subtle; it does not discern the sympathetic or antipathetic character (*nimitta*) of an object. Further, it belongs to a single species (*ekajātīya*). This along with uninterrupted series suggests that *ālaya-vijñāna* is in harmony with the sensation of indifference.[66] It has been further explained as follows:

---

62 Ganguly, 1992, op. cit., p. 83.

63 Ibid.

64 Balsys, 2006, *Karma and the Rebirth of Consciousness*, p. 2.

65 Ganguly, 1992, op. cit., p. 84.

66 Ibid.

> The sensation associated with the *ālaya-vijñāna* is pure retribution (*vipāka*) because it comes exclusively from the acts which have projected existence (*ākṣepaka karman*), without depending on actual conditions. Therefore, it is nothing, but the sensation of indifference. The two other sensations of joy and suffering are not "retributions", but born of retribution (*vipākaja*), because they depend on actual conditions, i.e. sympathetic and antipathetic objects.[67]

MANAS: NATURE AND ITS ACTIVITY

Manas (*manana-vijñāna* or thinking consciousness) manifests itself with *ālaya-vijñāna* as its support and makes *ālaya-vijñāna* as its object.[68] This is quite different from the Vedāntic position in which the mind happens to be the instrument in the manifestation of pure consciousness. However, *manas* in Buddhism is different from *mano-vijñāna*, but it is like *antaḥkaraṇa* (internal organ).[69] It may be noted that *ālaya-vijñāna* exists due to internal causation as mentioned earlier. Therefore, *manas* too works internally with *ālaya-vijñāna*. It is also observed that *manas* works as mediation between *ālaya-vijñāna* and *pravṛtti-vijñāna* (active consciousness).[70] *Manas* is referred to as self-consciousness which is caused entirely from within by the working of "unconscious" namely, *ālaya-vijñāna*.[71] The following comments regarding the origin of *manas* may be worth noting:

> The cause as condition of *manas* is the thing-in-itself aspect of store-consciousness. *Manas* is born from a seed of coveting a portion of the store-consciousness. The condition for development of *manas* is the perceiver aspect of store-consciousness. *Manas* is determined to hold on to the perceiver

[67] Ganguly, 1992, op. cit., p. 84.

[68] Ibid., p. 43.

[69] Acharya Narendradeva, 2001, *Baudha Dharma Darshan*, p. 464.

[70] Chatterjee, 1999, op. cit., p. 101.

[71] Kochumuttom, 1999, *A Buddhist Doctrine of Experience*, p. 97.

aspect of store-consciousness.[72]

Manas is continuously practising of cogitation (*manana*). In that it is different from the other consciousness. However, "*manas* is active in the *dhātu* or *bhūmi* in which sentient being is born and to which he is bound".[73] When the *manas* is involved in the transformation of *ālaya-vijñāna*, known as *pravṛtti-vijñāna* (active consciousness) the following four defilements (*kleśas*) start operating. These are given below:

i. Self-ignorance (*ātma-moha*): It creates an illusion regarding the true character of the *Ātman*, which is treated as false belief with regard to the concept of no-self (*nairātmya*).

ii. Self-belief (*ātma-dṛṣṭi*): It takes the *dharmas* as self, when the fact is that the *dharmas* are not self.

iii. Self-pride (*ātma-māna*): The belief in *Ātman* makes the mind feel superior.

iv. Self-love (*ātma-sneha*): The belief in the *Ātman* develops deep attachment to the self.

These four *kleśas* disturb and pollute the *ālaya-vijñāna* and cause the defilement in the *pravṛtti-vijñāna*. "This makes the sentient beings get lost in the cycle of birth and death, and are unable to escape from it. Therefore these are called defilements."[74]

In the state of arhatship, the above defilements are completely annihilated in both actual and *bīja* forms. Similar is the case with *nirodha-samāpatti* and in ascetic practices in the *lokottara-mārga*. "In both states *manas* does not exist."[75]

PRAVṚTTI-VIJÑĀNA

Ālaya-vijñāna provides a support (*āśrayakara*) through *manas* for

---

[72] Hanh, 2008, op. cit., pp. 102-03.

[73] Ganguly, 1992, op. cit., p. 44.

[74] Ibid., p. 91.

[75] Ibid., p. 44.

manifesting the cognitive awareness by appropriating the sense faculties.[76] This cognitive awareness is known as *pravṛtti-vijñāna*. It is stated that:

> Each moment of cognitive awareness is itself a resultant state, an effect of past *karma*, in other words, a fruitation of a seed. The ongoing and underlying processes that comprise the *ālaya-vijñāna* continuously condition the arising of supraliminal cognitive processes insofar as they store or "preserve" the specific causal conditions, the seeds, for these resultant processes to arise.[77]

Ālaya-vijñāna is the root consciousness from which all pure and impure consciousness are manifesting. Five sense consciousnesses — visual consciousness, auditory consciousness, olfactory consciousness, gustatory consciousness, tactile consciousness and mental consciousness — take the *ālaya-vijñāna* as their common and immediate support.

All five sense consciousnesses are treated as external because they give information about the external world.[78] However, in another source, the sense consciousnesses are treated as both: internal as well as external. It is observed that "visual consciousness is internal, while the eye is external; Similarly, auditory consciousness is internal, while the ear external; olfactory consciousness is internal, while the nose is external; gustatory consciousness is internal, while the tongue is external; tactile consciousness is internal, while the body is external."[79] The mental consciousness is certainly internal because it provides support in the manifestation of *ālaya-vijñāna*. This mental consciousness (*mano-vijñāna*) should not be confused with *manas*, because *manas* deliberates whereas *mano-vijñāna* discriminates.[80]

---

[76] Waldron, 2003, *The Buddhist Unconscious*, p. 112.

[77] Ibid., pp. 112-13.

[78] Chatterjee, 1999, op. cit., p. 106.

[79] Chang, 1983, *A Treasury of Mahāyāna Sūtras*, p. 227.

[80] Ganguly, 1992, op. cit., p. 44.

Pravṛtti-vijñānas are basically empirical ones and are involved in the world affairs. These are different consciousnesses, the unity among them is, however, provided by *ālaya-vijñāna* (i.e. store-consciousness). This is mainly because all these consciousnesses arise out of the storehouse consciousness (*ālaya-vijñāna*) by using their respective seeds stored in *ālaya-vijñāna*. The concept of *pravṛtti-vijñānas* arising out of stored-consciousness may be compared with the emergence of waves in the ocean. The *pravṛtti-vijñānas* are like waves, whereas the *ālaya-vijñāna* happens to be like the ocean.

It thus emerges that the objective cognitions (*pravṛtti-vijñānas*) are not due to external objects, but they are due to the maturation of subconscious impressions (*vāsanā paripāka*) within the stream consciousness itself. In this context it is stated that:

> Sub-conscious impressions are awakened by those antecedent mental states with which they are associated in the past and are raised to the level of consciousness. The revival of sub-conscious impressions is responsible for the emergence of object cognitions or sensations. They cannot be traced to external objects. Sensations are not "given". They are creations of the mind. The Yogācāra advocates unadulterated, subjectivism or mentalism.[81]

This kind of mentalism, however, does not find place in Sāṁkhya and Vedānta philosophies which treat the world as real "in the sense that it has objective existence for, and is not a projection of, the individual mind. In all such systems, Mind and Matter coexist."[82]

Even Sautrāntika Buddhists also believe in the existence of external objects. They argue that "the series of self-cognitions (*ālaya-vijñānas*) is uniformally present. But object-cognitions (*pravṛtti-vijñānas*) appear occasionally. Therefore, they must depend on something other than the series of self-cognitions. They are caused by external objects which are independent of all

---

[81] Sinha, 1999, *Indian Realism*, pp. 41-42.

[82] Woodroffe, 2001, *The World as Power*, p. 306.

cognitions."[83]

Ālaya-Vijñāna and Momentariness

Ālaya-vijñāna "is the ever-changing dynamic 'link' like the subterranean current of water in the ocean: the *Triṁśikā* calls it *dhruva* 'an ever-changing constant' (verse 30). It is ever-changing ever lastingness".[84] However, the changes are momentary. Each moment on the basis of the Buddha statement has three sub-moments: arising (*uppāda*), presence (*thiti*) and dissolution (*bhaṅga*).[85] These three sub-moments are misinterpreted by the Sautrāntikas by saying that "it is the series that Blessed One means to designate as conditioned; for quite clearly he does not attribute the three marks to each moment of the series".[86]

According to the Sautrāntikas there are only two sub-moments: arising and passing away, which form the momentary series. The first sub-moment (i.e. arising) gets destroyed completely; nothing is left in this preceding moment. Once destroyed, the new entity has come in its place. The latter may be similar to the former, but not the same. This happens to be "the doctrine of universal-momentariness, the point, where there remains no being but only becoming".[87]

In such momentary homogeneous series two things are happening: (i) in the complete destruction of the preceding sub-moment before the succeeding sub-moment, there is no time for any activity to leave its impressions. As a result, it may not be possible to accumulate impressions in the storehouse of consciousness, which is known as the *ālaya-vijñāna*; and (ii) being a homogeneous series, it may not be possible to arise the *karma* because the *karma*

---

[83] Sinha, 1999, op. cit., p. 39.

[84] Matilal, 1997, op. cit., p. 346.

[85] Bhikkhu Bodhi, 1999, *A Comprehensive Manual of Abhidhamma*, p. 156.

[86] Pruden, 1991, *Abhidharmakośabhāṣyam*, vol. I, p. 241.

[87] Kher, 1992, *Buddhism as Presented by the Brahmanical Systems*, p. 16.

is specific and particularized job.[88] The problem of circularity is also involved in this series.

In relation to cause and effect, the following observation may be noted:

> If effect is supposed to be produced from a cause that has become defunct, the effect will be destitute of a cause as defunct entity is a pure non-entity. And if it be conceived to be originated by a living cause, the cause must be conceded to exist for more than one moment. So the Buddhist is placed between horns of a dilemma. If he admits the former alternative, he cannot explain causation; if the latter alternative is accepted, he gives up his doctrine of universal flux.[89]

The observation on the unity of consciousness generated by the homogeneous series is equally intriguing. It is stated that "in reality, however, our consciousness does not possess unity at all; it is nothing but an ever-flowing unimpeded procession of unique conscious moments, each sharply divided from the other. The unity of consciousness is only illusion, generated by the homogeneity of the conscious units coupled with their uninterrupted career, their ceaseless continuum, which experiences no check and never comes to an abrupt end."[90] However, the fact is that consciousnesses itself comes to us with a unified structure. Kant called this unity as the transcendental unity of self-consciousness as mentioned earlier.

How to reconcile the above critical observation within the existing momentary framework? Some light may be thrown by examining the cause–effect relationship in each instant moment as explained by the Buddhist scholars like Diṅnāga, Dharmakīrti and Hsuan-tsang. We hope that their observations will help us to reconcile the above criticisms of the momentary homogeneous series.

---

[88] Balsys, 2006, op. cit., p. 4.

[89] Mookerjee, 1993, *The Buddhist Philosophy of Universal Flux*, p. 62.

[90] Ibid., pp. 82-83.

RECONCILIATION

The relationship between the preceding moments as cause to the succeeding moment is known as *samānāntara-pratyaya*. This requires the atomic data (a gross body, such as a table, may be thought of as an atom cluster) to emerge at a point instant simultaneously and without gaps to disappear at the next moment.[91] Since atoms being substantially or ultimately reality can cause the corresponding consciousness.[92] But it has been argued by Diṅnāga as follows:

> The atoms being formless themselves cannot contribute the form or image to the corresponding cognitive state.[93] For this purpose Diṅnāga developed the doctrine of self-consciousness (*svasaṁvitti*). The moment instant consists of not only two forms: comprehension (*grāhaka*) and comprehensible (*grāhya*), but it also includes self-consciousness in which both forms are revealed. "Self-cognition is a kind of mental perception which constitutes an integral part of each episode of awareness. Each episode of awareness in the consciousness series is ultimately real and self-revealing character, while it reveals both the object form and its comprehension."[94]

The above observation may be further supported by Dharmakīrti's explanation based on the principle of self-cognition. "Every cognition of an external object is at the same time a cognition of that cognition. Every feeling and every volition are, on the one side, connected with some object, but they also are, on the other side, self-conscious. We are thus possessed of an "awareness of our awareness".[95]

On the basis of above observation, an inference has been drawn that "in each event of awareness, according to the doctrine of self-

---

[91] Matilal, 1997, op. cit., p. 225.

[92] Ibid., p. 236.

[93] Ibid.

[94] Ibid., p. 237.

[95] Stcherbatsky, 1996, op. cit., vol. I, p. 163.

cognition, there are three aspects: the object aspect, its cognition and self-awareness (cf. *grāhya, grāhaka* and *svasaṁvitti*). All the three are internal parts of one momentary state of consciousness".[96] Now the question arises, how our different cognitive states would be accounted for? This may be explained not by the external world but by our internal impression (*vāsanā*), our mental dispositions, the residual forces of our past actions coupled with an ingrained beginningless ignorance.[97] It may be noted that self-cognition and self-consciousness are the same.

It is thus evident from the above observations that without admitting the doctrine of self-cognition and its appearance into object aspect and self-awareness aspect in a moment instant, it is difficult to account for recollection caused by memory impression of a past experience. According to Diṅnāga, unless a cognition is self-cognized, it can never be recollected.[98] Once self-cognition is admitted, each moment-instant itself becomes unity because it contains both: object appearance and cognition appearance. This may be supported by another observation which states that in cognition three elements: pure consciousness, an object and sense organ — are involved.[99] Pure consciousness is here referred to as self-cognition. These observations indicate that each cognition is self-cognized.

The doctrine of self-cognition is, however, criticized by Kumārila on the ground that the cognition cannot be both: the cognizer and the cognized. It is stated that "if the momentary cognition reveals itself to itself, it must take such form as 'I am blue', instead of 'this is blue'. But we find that a cognition always appears as pointing to 'this' which is other than itself. The functioning of cognition is directed outwards (*parāvṛtti*) and not inwards (*pratyāvṛtti*) as the

[96] Matilal, 1997, op. cit., p. 238.

[97] Ibid.

[98] Ibid., p. 243.

[99] Stcherbatsky, 1996, op. cit., vol. I, p. 173.

idealist theory implies. Therefore, the identity of the cognizer and the cognized is impossible."[100] In reply to this, Diṅnāga has said that "this theory leads to an infinite regress because to make recollection possible the second piece of cognition must be recognized by third piece of cognition and so ad infinitum".[101] Jayanta has also criticized the doctrine of self-cognition because it is not self-luminous. Therefore, it is not an acceptable theory.[102] Whatever may be the criticism of self-cognition, the fact remains that this is the most important contribution of Buddhist logicians.

The concept of self-consciousness has, however, been justified by Sartre a realist philosopher of the twentieth century. He has stated:

> The necessary and sufficient condition for a knowing consciousness to be knowledge of its object, is that it to be consciousness of itself as being that knowledge. This is necessary condition, for if my consciousness were not consciousness of being consciousness of the table, it would then be consciousness of that table without consciousness of being so. In other words, it would be a consciousness ignorant of itself, an unconscious, which is absurd. This is a sufficient condition.[103]

Now coming back to the cause and effect relationship in the moment-instant, it may be explained in a better way by taking into consideration the Chinese version of the *Treatise on Thirty Verses* (*Triṁśikā*) of Vasubandhu. According to Hsuan-tsang, when consciousness is born, its manifestation has two aspects: (i) the perceiving (*darśana*), and (ii) the perceived (*nimitta*) portions. The former discriminates the seeming subject (what can cause), and the latter is discriminated, the seeming object (what is caused). However, there is another functional aspect of consciousness that

---

[100] Bhatt, 1989, *The Basic Ways of Knowing*, pp. 35-36.

[101] Matilal, 1997, op. cit., p. 243.

[102] Ibid., p. 244.

[103] Sartre, 1984, *Being and Nothingness*, p. 11.

supports the perceiving and perceived divisions. "This is called self-corroboratory aspect (*svasaṁvitti-bhāga*). It is the realization by the consciousness of itself. If this was lacking, there would be no way of remembering the various manifestations of mind and its activities."[104] This implies that all three portions of consciousness operate simultaneously in the moment-instant. As a result, the moment-instant becomes complete in itself and forms unity because both: subject and object as cause and effect respectively are included in it.

Dividing consciousness into different portions is an absurdity, because consciousness in any way cannot be divided. But looking into at the problem seriously from the empirical point of view, this division into different manifestations provides a better understanding of the self-consciousness. It could be fairly compared with the concept of pre-reflective and reflective consciousness as developed by Sartre. The pre-reflective consciousness is comparable to perceiving (*darśana*) portion. Whereas the perceived (*nimitta*) portion may be compared with the reflective consciousness. The pre-reflective consciousness is the cause of the reflective consciousness which in a way is the effect of the former.

It emerges quite clearly from the above discussion that each moment-instant contains not only subject and object, which are treated as cause and effect, respectively, but also another functional aspect of consciousness that supports the perceiving and the perceived aspects. This is known as the self-corroborating aspect (*svasaṁvitti-bhāga*) under which both subject and object are revealed. Each point-instant in the consciousness series turns out to be ultimately real. Since each point-instant includes subject and object, i.e. cause and effect, it becomes unity in itself. When the consciousness series are formed on the basis of such point-instants, each point-instant becomes a bead in the chain. Further, such series may turn out to be heterogeneous rather than homogeneous one.

---

[104] Ganguly, 1992, op. cit., p. 139, note portion.

However, the criticism of the homogeneous series under which *karma* does not arise, because it is particularized job, will not be applicable to the suggested approach in which each point-instant will be an independent unit and it will differ from another point-instant. In this case, the series in all probability may turn out to be heterogeneous.

The above suggestion may be supported by Sartre's observation that the momentary instants of consciousness are unity in itself. It is stated that "each instant of consciousness is new existence, which does not arise out of prior instant. The rapid succession of instants constitutes one stream of experience. The instants are unified."[105] This unity is, however, treated as real and it is called the "unity within duration".[106]

[105] Medhidhammaporn, 1995, *Sartre's Existentialism and Early Buddhism*, p. 21.

[106] Ibid., pp. 21-22.

Epilogue

Solutions to the explanatory gap in the phenomenal consciousness and the mind–body problem of the Western philosophy have been provided in this study on the basis of not only philosophical observations available in the East–West perspective, but also on account of the scientific facts and reasonings.

The explanatory gap in the phenomenal consciousness in the Western philosophy arises mainly because the distinction between the consciousness itself and the functions of consciousness which may be referred to the consciousness for itself has not been made. The consciousness itself and its functions or manifestations are discussed separately in the Western philosophy. Whereas the fact is that the consciousness itself, when it manifests through the mind, according to the Vedānta school of the Indian philosophy, it becomes many as thinker, knower and perceiver in the phenomenal world, may be referred to as the relative existence of human beings. But here it should be recognized that the consciousness itself and its functions are not different but they are one and the same thing. This is mainly because the functional consciousness or phenomenal consciousness depends upon the consciousness itself, which is self-consciousness (self) embodied in human beings.

Similar is the case with the existentialism of Jean-Paul Sartre. The reflective consciousness depends on the pre-reflective consciousness. It may, however, be pointed out that the pre-reflective consciousness and reflective consciousness are not two different consciousnesses, but both are two different phases of the one and the same consciousness. Therefore, it may be said that the phenomenal consciousness is merely a reflection of self-consciousness. If this pathway of reflection is not accepted, it would be all the more difficult to solve the problem of explanatory gap in the phenomenal consciousness.

In the Western philosophy, the phenomenal consciousness has been explained through higher-order thought (HOT) by Rosenthal. It may be mentioned here that the thought being the object of consciousness cannot explain satisfactorily the phenomenal consciousness. However, the phenomenal consciousness may be explained through self-consciousness itself. It may be supported by Sartre's observation: "Since we know that nothing except consciousness can be the source of consciousness".[1] This is the reason for suggesting the pathway of reflection of consciousness seems to be the most appropriate approach to explain the phenomenal consciousness.

Those philosophers who have raised the problem of explanatory gap in the phenomenal consciousness have also discussed the access consciousness. If they would have taken seriously the access consciousness, the explanatory gap in the phenomenal consciousness would have been resolved easily. However, according to Sartre the access consciousness is real because it is easily accesssible to every human being. Therefore, it may be said that the phenomenal consciousness is the reflection of the access consciousness. In this approach there is no explanatory gap in the phenomenal consciousness.

Sartre has solved the mind–body problem in a unique way. He has tried to relate the body with consciousness. This is mainly because the other becomes the object for me and I become the object for others. In that, people wanted to link my consciousness of objects to the body of other. However, the other fact is that Sartre

---

[1] Sartre, 2012, *The Transcendence of the Ego*, p. 15.

has included the mind with the body itself. Therefore, there is no body–mind problem in the existentialism of Sartre. This is mainly because the mind is included in the human body itself.

The consciousness is embodied in human beings. Since it works through mind, it becomes self-consciousness according to Vedānta. However, according to Sartre also, all consciousness is self-consciousness. This is mainly because consciousness, while knowing the objects, knows itself. There is no other entity except self-consciousness in the entire universe which knows itself. In fact, without having conscious state, one cannot even negate consciousness. The embodied consciousness in human beings is also referred to as a representation which seems to have been started by the Indian philosophy of Buddhism.

The concept of *ālaya-vijñāna* of the Yogācāra Vijñānavāda school of Buddhism has representation of four aspects of consciousness. These are already mentioned in Chapter 7. What is important here is the *viṣaya-vijñapti* (objects as representation of consciousness). When it manifests, it becomes the phenomenal consciousness. There is, therefore, no problem at all in explaining the phenomenal consciousness in Yogācāra Vijñānavāda of Buddhism.

Searle has solved the mind–body problem through the unity of consciousness, which happens to be the first-person ontology, because it cannot be reduced to neurological basis. All experiences are part of a single unity of conscious field, which comes to us with a unified structure. Kant called this unity of conscious field the transcendental unity of apperception.

What is the most important is that even the quantum physics has provided the solution to the mind–body problem. In this context, it is observed that mind and matter are different projections from the deeper implicate order, where such a division does not exist. This reassures that the implicate order provides the solution to the mind–body problem.

The scientific concept of the mental state as physical one is known as the materialism. This has been started from the ancient Greece. The elementary particles were ultimate indestructible units of the matter in the Democritean sense. The material atoms alone account for the whole universe. This may, however, be supported by the Vedic vision according to which even consciousness grows out of matter when it becomes organic. The materialism may, further, be justified on two accounts: (i) the matter has been dematerialized over the period of time and now it is identified with energy; and (ii) the matter is basically causation. Both are stated below:

(i) Energy is inseparably associated with matter and matter inseparably associated with energy. Similarly, mind is inseparably coupled with matter and matter with mind, their unity being found in the power of consciousness which is neither and which transcends both.[2]

(ii) For matter is absolutely nothing but causality. . . . Its being is its acting; it is not possible to conceive for it any other being. Only as something acting does it fill space and time; its action on the immediate object (which is itself matter) conditions the perception in which alone it exists. The consequence of the action of every material object on another is known only in so far as the latter now acts on the immediate object in way different from that in which acted previously; it consists in this alone. Thus cause and effect are the whole essence and nature of matter. . . . Its whole being and essence consist only in the orderly and regular change produced by one part of it in another; consequently, its being and essence are entirely relative.[3]

Now let us see how the mind–body problem has been solved in the Indian philosophy. In the Sāṁkhya–Yoga the mind–body problem gets solved mainly because the concept of *guṇas* — *sattva, rajas* and *tamas* — operates in both *prakṛti* and *puruṣa*. Therefore, the

---

[2] Woodroffe, 2001, *The World as Power*, pp. 182-83.

[3] Cross, 2014, *Schopenhauer's Encounter with Indian Thought*, p. 63.

distinction between the mind and body, subjective and objective, does not apply.

In the *Taittirīya Upaniṣad*, five *kośas* have been defined in a unique manner, shown through the hierarchy of entities. However, from the point view of the mind–body problem these *kośas* have been reinterpreted. In that, it may be stated that when the mind transcends to higher level, i.e. *Vijñānamaya* which is known as self-consciousness, it includes the mind along with *prāṇamaya* as body. In self-consciousness, both the mind and body get united. Therefore, it may be said that in self-consciousness the mind–body problem is resolved.

One thing that stands out quite clear in this study is that inner sense does exist. The dream experience itself is the proof of inner sense. In fact, inner sense and outer sense are inseparable. In self-consciousness inner sense and outer sense become one because the latter is the manifestation of the former. This is just opposite to Kant, who has pointed out that inner perception is known through outer perception.

In the identity theory the mind is treated as identical to brain. This theory does not seem to be appropriate in capturing the subtlety of cognition, which is known through the mind. This is evident from the following observation:

> The qualificand–qualifier distinction is relative and may vary depending on the nature of the cognition. If instead of the cognition that the rose is red, what is cognized is that the red color is in the rose, the red color becomes the qualificand and the rose or belonging to the rose, the qualifier. A situation may be described and cognized in two or five or ten or even more different ways and the distinction between the qualificand and the qualifier will vary accordingly. Such fluidity of the distinction is a chief reason for the privacy of cognitive states. The latter are private in the sense that only the cognizer knows what the content of cognition is. Additionally, only that person knows what precisely is the qualificand and the qualifier. Even if a third

person may make an intelligent guess about what roughly is the content, he may have no inkling of what exactly is the qualificand and the qualifier. The cognitive fluidity also provides a serious obstacle to many anti-dualist theories of the mind. Those who hold that cognitive states are identical with brain states, for example, have singularly failed to show that there are actually ten different brain states corresponding to ten different descriptions and cognitions of a situation. In fact, the most advanced and detailed study of what is happening in the brain has yielded no clue as to what precisely is the qualificand or the qualifier of a particular cognition of a particular person at a particular time.[4]

[4] Chakrabarti, 2001, *Classical Indian Philosophy of Mind*, p. 32.

Bibliography

Acharya Narendradeva, 2001, *Baudha Dharma Darshan*, Delhi: Motilal Banarsidass.

Adhvarindra, D., 2000, *Vedanta Paribhasa*, tr. Swami Madhavananda, Calcutta: Advaita Ashrama.

Aung, S.Z., 1979, *Compendium of Philosophy*, London: The Pali Text Society.

Balasubramanian, R., 2004, "Advaita Vedānta on the Problem of Enworlded Subjectivity", in *Phenomenology and Indian Philosophy*, ed. D.P. Chattopadhyaya, L. Embree and J. Mohanty, New Delhi: Indian Council of Philosophical Research.

Balsekar, R.S., 1999, *Pointers from Nisargadatta Maharaj*, Bombay: Chetana.

Balslev, A.N., 1999, *A Study of Time in Indian Philosophy*, New Delhi: Munshiram Manoharlal.

Balsys, B., 2006, *Karma and the Rebirth of Consciousness*, New Delhi: Munshiram Manoharlal.

——, 2013, *The Enigma of Consciousness*, New Delhi: Oxford University Press.

Bart, W.H., 1995, *Philosophy of Knowledge*, vols I and II, ed. H.L. Mansel and John Veitch, Delhi: Ajay Book Service.

Besant, A., 2000, *Man and His Bodies*, Chennai: The Theosophical Publishing House.

Bhadra, M.K. 2004, *A Critical Survey of Phenomenology and Existentialism*, New Delhi: Indian Council of Philosophical Research.

Bhatt, G.P., 1989, *The Basic Ways of Knowing*, Delhi: Motilal Banarsidass.

Bhattacharya, K., 1992, *Advaitasiddhiḥ of Madhusūdana Sarasvatī*, New Delhi: Indian Council of Philosophical Research.

Bhattacharyya, K.C., 1983, *Studies in Philosophy*, ed. G. Bhattacharyya, Delhi: Motilal Banarsidass.

Bhattacharyya, S., 2009, "Molecules that Are Involved in Cellular Consciousness" in *Understanding Consciousness: Recent Advances*, ed. Swami Sarvabhutananda, papers read at a seminar held at the Ramakrishana Mission Institute of Culture, Kolkata on 19-20 January 2008.

Bhattacharyya, S., 2004, "Phenomenology and Indian Philosophy", in *Phenomenology and Indian Philosophy*, ed. D.P. Chattopadhyaya, Lestter Embree, Jitendranath Mohanty, New Delhi: Indian Council of Philosophical Research.

Bhaumik, M., 2005, *Code Name God: The Spiritual Odyssey of a Man of Science*, New Delhi: Penguin Books.

Bhikkhu Bodhi (gen. ed.), 1999, *A Comprehensive Manual of Abhidhamma: The Abhidhammattha of Ācariya Anuruddha*, Kandy, Sri Lanka: Buddhist Publication Society.

Block, N., 2002, "Concepts of Consciousness", in *Philosophy of Mind*, ed. D.J. Chalmers, New York and Oxford: Oxford University Press.

Block, N., O. Flanagan and G. Guzeldere (eds), 2002, *The Nature of Consciousness: Philosophical Debates*, Cambridge, MA: The MIT Press.

Bohm, D., 2012, *Wholeness and Implicate Order*, London and New York: Routledge.

Bohm, D. and F.D. Peat, 1987, *Science, Order and Creativity*, New York: Bantam Books.

Boisvert, M., 1997, *The Five Aggregates*, Delhi: Sri Satguru Publications.

Capra, F., 1989, *The Tao of Physics*, London: Fontana Paperbacks.

Catalina, F.V., 1968, *A Study of the Self: Concept of the Sāṁkhya-Yoga Philosophy*, Delhi: Munshiram Manoharlal.

Chakrabarti, K.K., 2001, *Classical Indian Philosophy of Mind: The Nyāya Dualist Tradition*, Delhi: Motilal Banarsidass.

Chakraborty, A., 1997, *Mind-Body Dualism*, New Delhi: D.K. Printworld.

Chalmers, D.J., 2002, *Philosophy of Mind: Classical and Contemporary Readings*, New York and Oxford: Oxford University Press.

Chang, G.C.C. (gen. ed.), 1983, *A Treasury of Mahāyāna Sūtras: Selection from the Mahāratnakūṭasūtra*, University Park and London: The Pennsylvania State University Press.

Chatterjee, A.K., 1999, *The Yogācāra Idealism*, Delhi: Motilal Banarsidass.

Chatterjee, T., S. Basu and A. Chatterjee, 2014, *J.N. Mohanty Lectures on Kant's Critiaque of Pure Reason*, New Delhi: Munshiram Manoharlal.

Chaudhury, S., 1983, *Analytical Study of the Abhidharmakośa*, Calcutta: Firma KLM.

Cross, S., 2014, *Schopenhauer's Encounter with Indian Thought*, New Delhi: Munshiram Manoharlal.

Datta, D.M., 1998, *The Six Ways of Knowing*, Calcutta: University of Calcutta.

Datt, N., 1978, *Mahāyāna Buddhism*, Delhi: Motilal Banarsidass.

Descartes, R., 2002, "Meditations on First Philosophy", in *Philosophy of Mind*, ed. D.J. Chalmers, New York: Oxford University Press.

Dretske, F., 2002, "Conscious Experience", in *Philosophy of Mind*, ed. D.J. Chalmers, New York and Oxford: Oxford University Press.

Dyczkowski, M.S.G., 2006, *The Doctrine of Vibration: An Analysis of the Doctrines and Practice of Kashmir Shaivism*, Delhi: Motilal Banarsidass.

Feinberg, T.E., 2001, *Altered Egos: How the Brain Creates the Self*, New York and Oxford: Oxford University Press.

Ganguly, S. (tr.), 1992, *Treatise in Thirty Verses on Mere Consciousness*, Delhi: Motilal Banarsidass.

Grimes, J., 1992, *The Naiṣkarmyasiddhi of Sureśvara: A Monograph*, Delhi: Sri Satguru Publications.

Haldar, A., 2001, *Some Psychological Aspects of Early Buddhist Philosophy Based on Abhidharmakośa of Vasubandhu*, Kolkata: The Asiatic Society.

Hanh, T., 2008, *Understanding Our Mind*, New Delhi: Harper Collins.

Hegel, G.W.F., 1998, *Phenomenology of Spirit*, tr. A.V. Miller, Delhi: Motilal Banarsidass.

Hoffe, O., 2010, *Kant's Critique of Pure Reason: The Foundation of Modern Philosophy*, London and New York: Springer.

Indich, W.M., 2000, *Consciousness in Advaita Vedānta*, Delhi: Motilal Banarsidass.

Jha, G. (tr.), 1986, *Tattvasaṁgraha of Śāntaraksita with Commentary of Kamalshila*, vol. II, Delhi: Motilal Banarsidass.

Joshi, M.M., 2006, "Life, Mind and Consciousness", in *Life, Mind and Consciousness*, Kolkata: The Ramakrishna Mission Institute of Culture.

Kalupahana, D.J., 1992, *The Principles of Buddhist Psychology*, Delhi: Sri Satguru Publications.

Kant, I., 1950, *The Critique of Pure Reason*, tr. J.M.D. Meiklejohn, London: Dent and Sons.

Kher, C.V., 1992, *Buddhism as Presented by the Brahmanical Systems*, Delhi: Sri Satguru Publications.

Kochumuttom, T.A., 1999, *A Buddhist Doctrine of Experience*, Delhi: Motilal Banarsidass.

Koestenbaum, P., 1971, "Religion in the Tradition of Phenomenology", in *Religion in Philosophical and Cultural Perspective*, ed. J.C. Flaver and W. Horosz, New Delhi: Affiliated East-West Press.

Kothari, D.S., 2002, "Atom and Self", in *Collection of Lectures Delivered by D.S. Kothari*, ed. F. Ahmad, New Delhi: New Age International.

Krishnamurti, J., 1992, *Choiceless Awareness*, California: Krishnamurti Foundation of America.

Larson, G.J. and R.S. Bhattacharya, 1987, *Encyclopedia of Indian Philosophy*, vol. IV: *Sāṁkhya*, Delhi: Motilal Banarsidass.

Levy, J., 2004, *The Nature of Man According to the Vedānta*, Boulder, CO: Sentient Publications.

Manju, 1986, *Advaitavāda aura Sūnyavāda* (Hindi), Delhi: Eastern Book Linkers.

Masih, Y., 2002, *A Critical History of Western Philosophy*, Delhi: Motilal Banarsidass.

Matilal, B.K., 1986, *Perception: An Essay on Classical Indian Theories of Knowledge*, Oxford: Clarendon Press.

——, 1997, *Logic, Language and Reality*, Delhi: Motilal Banarsidass.

Medhidhammaporn, P., 1995, *Sartre's Existentialism and Early Buddhism*, Bangkok: Buddhadhamma Foundation.

Merleau-Ponty, M., 2005, *Phenomenology of Perception*, New York: Routledge.

Mohanty, J.N., 1995, "Some Aspects of Indian Thinking on Being", in *The Question of Being: East–West Perspective*, ed. Sprung Mervyn, Delhi: Sri Satguru Publications.

Mookerjee, S., 1993, *The Buddhist Philosophy of Universal Flux*, Delhi: Motilal Banarsidass.

Mukerji, A.C., 1938, *The Nature of Self*, Allahabad: The Indian Press.

Nicholson, G.L., 1962, *Illustration of Being*, New Jersey: Humanities Press.

Panda, N.C., 2013, *Mind and Supermind*, vol. II, New Delhi: D.K. Printworld.

Pandit, M.L., 2008, *The Buddhist View of Knowledge and Reality*, New Delhi: Munshiram Manoharlal.

——, 2012, *The Philosophical and Practical Aspects of Kashmir Śaivism: A Study of Trika Thought and Practice*, New Delhi: Munshiram Manoharlal.

Potter, K.H., 1998, *Encyclopedia of Indian Philosophy*, vol. III: *Advaita Vedānta up to Śaṅkara and His Pupils*, Delhi: Motilal Banarsidass.

Powell, A.E., 2005, *The Causal Body and the Ego*, Adyar (Chennai): The Theosophical Publishing House.

Pruden, L.M. (tr.), 1991, *Abhidharmakośabhāṣyam*, vol. I by Louis La Vallée Poussin, Berkeley, CA: Asian Humanities Press.

Radhakrishnan, S., 1999, *Indian Philosophy*, vol. II, New Delhi: Oxford University Press.

——, 2009, *The Principal Upaniṣads*, New Delhi: Harper Collins.

Rajagopal, L.V., 1993, *A Critique of Vedānta*, New Delhi: Munshiram Manoharlal.

Ram, K., 1995, *Integral Non-Dualism*, Delhi: Motilal Banarsidass.

Reat, N.R., 1990, *Origins of Indian Psychology*, Berkeley, CA: Asian Humanities Press.

Rosenthal, D.M., 2002, "Explaining Consciousness", in *Philosophy of Mind*, ed. D. J. Chalmers, New York and Oxford: Oxford University Press.

——, 2005, *Consciousness and Mind*, New York: Oxford University Press.

Roy, K., 2013, *Subjectivity in Science: Interpretations of the Cartesian Project*, Kolkata: Ramakrishna Mission Institute of Culture.

Sadhu, Santinatha, 1938, *The Critical Examination of the Philosophy and Religion*, vol. II, Amalner: Pratap Seth.

Safaya, R., 1976, *Indian Psychology*, New Delhi: Munshiram Manoharlal.

Sarbadhikari, A., 1991, *Mill's Self Regarding Acts: An Analysis*, Shimla: Indian Institute of Advanced Study, in association with Munshiram Manoharlal, New Delhi.

Sartre, J.-P., 1962, *Imagination: A Psychological Critique*, tr. Forrest Williams, Ann Arbor: University of Michigan Press.

———, 1984, *Being and Nothingness*, tr. Hazel E. Barnes, New York: Washington Square Press.

——, 2012, *The Transcendence of the Ego*, Routledge Classics, first Indian Reprint.

Searle, J.R., 2004, *Mind: A Brief Introduction*, New York: Oxford University Press.

Sinari, R.K., 2007, *The Paradox of Being Human*, New Delhi: Indian Council of Philosophical Research.

Singh, S.P., 2004, *Vedic Vision of Consciousness and Reality*, New Delhi: PHISPC-Centre for Studies in Civilizations.

Sinha, J.N., 1999, *Indian Realism*, Delhi: Motilal Banarsidass.

Sinha, N.L., 2013, *The Sāṁkhya Philosophy*, New Delhi: Munshiram Manoharlal.

Sparham, G. and Shotara (trs), 1993, *Ocean of Eloquence: Tsongakhapa's Commentary on Yogācāra Doctrine of Mind*, New York: SUNY Press.

Sri Sri Paramahansa Yogananda, 2007, *The Bhagavad Gītā*, vol. I, Kolkata: Yogoda Satsanga Society of India.

Stcherbatsky, T. (tr.), 1978, *Madhyānta-Vibhaṅga*, vol. II, New Delhi: Oriental Books Reprint Corporation.

——, 1996, *Buddhist Logic*, vols I-II, New Delhi: Munshiram Manoharlal.

——, 2003, *The Conception of Buddhist Nirvana*, Delhi: Motilal Banarsidass.

Suzuki, D.T., 1999, *Studies in the Laṅkāvatārasūtra*, Delhi: Motilal Banarsidass.

Swami Bhajanananda, 2009, "Knowledge and Consciousness: An Integral Approach", in *Understanding Consciousness: Recent Advances*, ed. Swami Sarvabhutananda, Kolkata: Ramakrishna Mission Institute of Culture.

Swami Gambhirananda (tr.), 2000, *Brahmasūtrabhāṣya of Śrī Śaṅkarācārya*, Kolkata: Advaita Ashrama.

——— (tr.), 2004, *Taittirīya Upaniṣad with Commentary of Śaṅkarācārya*, Kolkata: Advaita Ashrama.

Swami Jagadananda (tr.), 2000, *Upadeśasāhasrī of Śri Śaṅkarācārya*, Madras: Sri Ramakrishna Math.

Swami Jitatmananda, 1993, *Holistic Science and Vedānta*, Bombay: Bhartiya Vidya Bhavan.

Swami Madhavananda (tr.), 1997, *The Bṛhadāraṇyaka Upaniṣad with Commentary of Śaṅkarācārya*, Calcutta: Advaita Ashrama.

Swami Mukhyananda, 2006, *Sri Shankaracharya: Life and Philosophy: An Elucidative and Reconciliatory Interpretation*, Kolkata: Advaita Ashrama.

Swami Muni Narayana Prasad, 1998, *Muṇḍaka Upaniṣad*, New Delhi: D.K. Printworld.

——, 2004, *Kaṭha Upaniṣad*, New Delhi: D.K. Printworld.

———, 2009a, *The Taittirīya Upaniṣad*, New Delhi: D.K. Printworld.

———, 2009b, *Īśāvāsya and Māṇḍūkya Upaniṣads*, New Delhi: D.K. Printworld.

Swami Nikhilananda (tr.), 1997, *Vedāntasāra*, Calcutta: Advaita Ashrama.

——— (tr.), 2000, *The Māṇḍūkya Upaniṣad with Gauḍapāda's Kārikā and Śaṅkara's Commentary*, Calcutta: Advaita Ashrama.

——— (tr.), 2008, *Self Knowledge of Śrī Śaṅkarācārya*, Chennai: Sri Ramakrishna.

Swami Ranganathananda, 2001, *The Message of the Upanishads*, Mumbai: Bhartiya Vidya Bhavan.

Swami Satprakashananda, 2001, *Methods of Knowledge*, Kolkata: Advaita Ashrama.

——, 2004, *The Universe God and God-Realization from the Viewpoint of Vedānta*, Chennai: Sri Ramakrisna Math.

Swami Satchidanandendra, 1997, *The Method of the Vedānta: A Critical Account of the Advaita Tradition*, tr. A.J. Alston, Delhi: Motilal Banarsidass.

Swami Swahananda (tr.), 2001, *Pañcadaśī of Sri Vidyaranya Swami*, Chennai: Sri Ramakrishna Math.

Swami Tattwananda (tr.), 2002, *The Quintessence of Vedānta of Śrī Śaṅkarācārya*, Kalady: Sri Ramakrishna Advaita Ashrama.

Swami Turiyananda (tr.), 2007, *Vivekacūḍāmaṇi of Śrī Śaṅkarācārya*, Chennai: Sri Ramakrishna Math.

Swami Virupakshananda (tr.), 2003, *Sāṁkhyakārikā of Īśvarakṛṣṇa*, Chennai: Sri Ramakrishna Math.

Swami Yogeshwaranand Saraswati, 1987, *Science of Soul*, Rishikesh: Yoga Niketan Trust.

Swami Yogindrananda (tr.), 2005, *Pramāṇavārtikam of Dharmakīrti*, vol. II, Varanasi: Chowkhamba Vidyabhawan.

Taimni, I.K., 1998, *The Secret of Self Realization*, Chennai: The Theosophical Publishing House.

——, 1999, *The Science of Yoga*, Chennai: The Theosophical Publishing House.

Thanh, T.M., 2008, *The Mind in Early Buddhism*, New Delhi: Munshiram Manoharlal.

Thibaut, G. (tr.), 1994, *The Vivaraṇaprameya-Saṁgraha of Vidyāraṇya*, Delhi: Sri Satguru Publications.

Thomas, V.C., 2004, "Husserlian Foundations of Sartre's Treatment of Time Consciousness", in *Phenomenology and Indian Philosophy*, ed. D.P. Chattopadhyaya, L. Embree and J. Mohanty, New Delhi: Indian Council of Philosophical Research.

Tilak, B.G., 2000, *Śrīmadbhagavadgītā : Gita-Rahasya (Hindi)*, Pune: Tilak Brothers.

Tola, F. and C. Dragonetti, 2004, *Being as Consciousness: Yogācāra Philosophy of Buddhism*, Delhi: Motilal Banarsidass.

Torella, R. and B. Bäumer 2016, *Utpaladeva: Philosopher of Recognition*, Shimla: Indian Institute of Advanced Study and New Delhi: D.K. Printworld.

Waldron, W.S., 2003, *The Buddhist Unconscious: The Ālaya-vijñāna, in the Context of Indian Buddhist Thought*, London and New York: Routledge–Curzon.

Warner, R. and T. Szubka (eds), 1994, *The Mind-Body Problem: A Guide to the Current Debate*, New Jersey, NJ: Blackwell.

Wilber, K., 1984, *Quantum Questions*, New York: Shambhala Publications.

Woodroffe, J., 2001, *The World as Power*, repr., Madras: Ganesh and Co.

Index